ITALIAN
PHRASEBOOK

**GEDDES&
GROSSET**

Published 2005 by Geddes & Grosset,
David Dale House, New Lanark ML11 9DJ, Scotland

© 1998 Geddes & Grosset,

First published 1998
Reprinted 1999, 2001, 2002, 2003, 2004, 2005

ISBN 1 85534 355 X

Printed and bound in Poland

POLSKABOOK

CONTENTS

CONTENTS

Contents

KEY TO PRONUNCIATION

Guide to Italian pronunciation scheme

Vowels

a	as a in b<u>a</u>d, f<u>a</u>ther
ay	as a in d<u>ay</u>
e	as e in b<u>e</u>d, fath<u>e</u>r
ee	as e in m<u>e</u>
y	as in b<u>i</u>t
o	as in h<u>o</u>t
oh	as in b<u>o</u>ne

Consonants

ch	as in <u>ch</u>at
k	as in <u>c</u>at
g	as in <u>g</u>et
j	as in <u>g</u>inger
ly	as in mi<u>lli</u>on
ny	as in compa<u>ni</u>on
h	is not pronounced
ts	as in ca<u>ts</u>
dz	as in ro<u>ds</u>

Hyphens are given to show syllables but should be ignored when speaking. The stressed syllable in a word is in bold type.

GETTING STARTED

Everyday words and phrases

Yes
Sì
see

Thank you
Grazie
gra-tsyay

No
No
no

Good
Bene
bay-nay

OK
Va bene
va bay-nay

Excuse me
Mi scusi
mee skoo-zi

Please
Per piacere
payr pya-chay-ray

Excuse me, please
Mi scusi, per favore
mee skoo-zi, payr fa-voh-ray

Yes, please
Sì, grazie
see, gra-tsyay

I am very sorry
Mi dispiace molto
mee dees-pyah-chay mohl-toh

Being understood

I do not understand
Non capisco
nohn ka-pee-skoh

I do not speak Italian
Non parlo italiano
nohn par-loh ee-tal-yah-noh

Can you find someone who speaks English?
Può trovare qualcuno che parla inglese?
pwo troh-vah-ray kwal-koo-noh kay par-la een-glay-zay

Can you help me, please?
Mi può aiutare, per favore?
mee pwo a-yoo-tah-ray, payr fa-voh-ray

Please repeat that slowly
Per favore, ripeta più lentamente
payr fa-voh-ray, ree-pay-ta pyoo layn-ta-mayn-tay

It does not matter
Non importa
nohn eem-por-ta

Who speaks English?
Chi parla inglese?
kee pahr-la een-glay-zay?

Greetings and exchanges

Hello
Ciao
chao

Hi
Ciao
chao

Good morning
Buon giorno
bwon johr-noh

Good night
Buona notte
bwo-na not-tay

Goodbye
Arrivederci
ar-ree-vay-dayr-chee

Good evening
Buona sera
bwo-na say-ra

How are you?
Come sta?
koh-may sta

I am very well, thank you
Sto bene, grazie
stoh bay-nay, grats-yay

My name is…
Mi chiamo…
mee kyah-moh

What is your name?
Come si chiama?
koh-may see kyah-ma

Here is my son
Questo è mio figlio
kwe-stoh e mee-oh fee-lyoh

This is — my daughter
Questa è — mia figlia
kwe-sta e — mee-a fee-lya

— my wife
— mia moglie
— mee-a moh-lyay

This is — my husband
Questo è — mio marito
kwe-sto e — mee-oh ma-ree-toh

Greetings and exchanges

I am a student
Sono studente
*soh-noh stoo-**den**-tay*

I am from America
Sono americano / americana
*soh-noh a-may-ree-**kah**-noh / a-may-ree-**kah**-nah*

I am from Australia
Sono australiano / australiana
*soh-noh a-oo-stra-**lya**-noh / a-oo-stra-**lya**-nah*

I am from Canada
Sono canadese
*soh-noh ka-nu-**day**-zay*

I am from England
Sono inglese
*soh-noh een-**glay**-zay*

I am from Ireland
Sono irlandese
*soh-noh eer-lan-**day**-zay*

I am from New Zealand
Sono neo-zelandese
*soh-noh **nay**-oh-dzay-lan-**day**-zay*

I am from Scotland
Sono scozzese
*soh-noh skot-**tsay**-zay*

I am from South Africa
Sono sudafricano / sudafricana
*soh-noh soo-da-free-**kah**-noh / soo-da-free-**kah**-nah*

I am from Wales
Sono gallese
*soh-noh gal-**lay**-zay*

I am on holiday
Sono in vacanza
*soh-noh een va-**kan**-tsa*

I live in London
Abito a Londra
*a-bee-toh a **lohn**-dra*

It is good to see you
Sono contento di vederla
*soh-noh kohn-**ten**-toh dee vay-**dayr**-la*

It is nice to meet you
Molto lieto
***mohl**-toh **lye**-toh*

That is very kind of you
Lei è molto gentile
*le-ee e **mohl**-toh jayn-**tee**-lay*

You are very kind
Lei è molto gentile
*le-ee e **mohl**-toh jayn-**tee**-lay*

13

Asking questions

You are very welcome!
Si figuri
*see fee-**goo**-ree*

See you soon
Arrivederci a presto
*ar-ree-vay-**dayr**-chee a **pre**-stoh*

Asking questions

Where?
Dove?
***doh**-vay*

Where is?
Dov'è?
doh-ve

Where are?
Dove sono?
***doh**-vay **soh**-noh*

When?
Quando?
***kwan**-doh*

What?
Che?
kay

How?
Come?
***koh**-may*

How much?
Quanto?
***kwan**-toh*

Who?
Chi?
kee

Why?
Perché?
***payr**-kay*

Which?
Cosa? / Quale?
***ko**-za / **kwah**-lay*

Common questions

Do you mind if I . . . ?
Le dispiace se . . . ?
lay dee-spyah-chay say . . .

Have you got any change?
Ha moneta?
a moh-nay-ta

How long will it take?
Quanto ci vorrà?
kwan-toh chee vor-ra

May I borrow your map?
Mi può prestare la sua carta?
mee pwo pray-stah-ray la soo-a kar-ta

What is the problem?
Che problema c'è?
kay proh-ble-ma che

What is this?
Che cos'è questo?
kay ko-ze kwe-sto

What is wrong?
Che cosa c'è che non va?
kay ko-za che kay nohn va

Common questions

What time do you close?
A che ora chiudete?
*a kay **oh**-ra kyoo-**day**-tay*

Where can I buy a postcard?
Dove posso comprare delle cartoline?
*doh-vay **pos**-soh cohm-**prah**-ray **del**-lay kar-toh-**lee**-nay*

Where can I buy currency?
Dove posso cambiare dei soldi?
*doh-vay **pos**-soh kam-**byah**-ray **day**-ee **sol**-dee*

Where can I change my clothes?
Dove posso cambiarmi?
*doh-vay **pos** soh kam-**byahr**-mee*

Where can I change traveller's cheques?
Dove posso cambiare dei traveller's cheques?
*doh-vay **pos**-soh kam-**byah**-ray **day**-ee **tra**-vayl-layrs cheks*

Where is the toilet?
Dov'è la toilette?
*doh-**ve** la toh-ee layt-ta (twa-**let**)*

Who did this?
Chi l'ha fatto?
*kee la **fat**-toh*

Who should I see about this?
Con chi devo parlare per questo?
*kohn kee **day**-voh par-**lah**-ray payr **kwe**-stoh*

Will you come?
Verrà?
*ver-**ra***

Asking the time

What time is it?
Che ora è?
*kay **oh**-ra e*

   It is —
   Sono le —
***soh**-noh lay —*

        — eleven o'clock
        — undici
        — ***oon**-dee-chee*

        — ten o' clock
        — dieci
        — ***dye**-chee*

        — twelve o'clock
        — dodici
        — ***doh**-dee-chee*

        — a quarter past ten
        — dieci e un quarto
        — *dye-chee ay oon **kwahr**-toh*

17

Asking the time

— **a quarter to eleven**
— dieci e tre quarti
— *dye-chee ay tray **kwahr**-tee*

— **five past ten**
— dieci e cinque
— *dye-chee ay **cheen**-kway*

— **five to eleven**
— undici meno cinque
— ***oon**-dee-chee **may**-noh **cheen**-kway*

— **half past eight exactly**
— otto e mezza precise
— ***ot**-toh ay **med**-za pray-**chee**-say*

— **half past ten**
— dieci e mezza
— *dye-chee ay **med**-za*

— **ten past ten**
— dieci e dieci
— *dye-chee ay **dye**-chee*

— **ten to eleven**
— undici meno dieci
— ***oon**-dee-chee **may**-noh **dye**-chee*

— **after three o'clock**
— dopo le tre
— ***doh**-poh lay tre*

— **nearly five o'clock**
— quasi le cinque
— *kwa-zee lay **cheen**-kway*

— **twenty past ten**
— dieci e venti
— *dye-chee ay **vayn**-tee*

— **twenty-five past ten**
— dieci e venticinque
— *dye-chee ay vayn-tee-**cheen**-kway*

— **twenty to eleven**
— dieci e quaranta
— *dye-chee ay kwa-**ran**-ta*

— **twenty-five to eleven**
— dieci e trentacinque
— *dye-chee ay trayn-ta-**cheen**-kway*

It is — **early**
É — presto
*e — **pre**-stoh*

— **late**
— tardi
— *tar-dee*

— **midday**
— mezzogiorno
— *med-zoh-**johr**-noh*

Asking the time

— midnight
— mezzanotte
— *med-za-**not**-tay*

before midnight
prima di mezzanotte
*pree-ma dee med-za-**not**-tay*

at about one o'clock
verso l'una / verso le una
*vayr-soh **loo**-na / **vayr**-soh lay **oo**-na*

at half past six
alle sei e mezza
*al-lay se-ee ay **med**-za*

in an hour's time
fra un'ora
*fra oon-**oh**-ra*

in half an hour
tra mezz'ora
*tra med-**zoh**-ra*

at night
di notte
*dee **not**-tay*

soon
presto
pre-stoh

this afternoon
questo pomeriggio
*kwe-stoh poh-may-**reej**-joh*

this evening
questa sera / stasera
*kwe-sta **say**-ra / tsa-**say**-ra*

this morning
questa mattina / stamattina
*kwe-sta mat-**tee**-na / sta-mat-**tee**-na*

tonight
stanotte
*sta-**not**-tay*

two hours ago
due ore fa
***doo**-ay **oh**-ray fa*

Common problems

I cannot find my driving licence
Non riesco a trovare la patente
*nohn ree-e-skoh a troh-**vah**-ray la pa-**ten**-tay*

I have dropped a contact lens
Ho perso una lente a contatto
*oh **per**-soh **oo**-na **len**-tay a kohn-**tat**-toh*

21

Common problems

I have lost my credit cards
Ho perso le mie carte di credito
*oh **per**-soh lay **mee**-ay **kar**-tay dee **cray**-dee-toh*

I have lost my key
Ho perso la chiave
*oh **per**-soh la **kyah**-vay*

I have lost my ticket
Ho perso il biglietto
*oh **per**-soh eel bee-**lyayt**-toh*

I have lost my traveller's cheques
Ho perso i travellers' cheques
*oh **per**-soh ee **tra**-vayl-layrs cheks*

I have no currency
Non ho soldi italiani
*nohn oh **sol**-dee ee-ta-**lyah**-nee*

I haven't enough money
Non ho abbastanza soldi
*nohn oh ab-ba-**stant**-sa **sol**-dee*

My car has been stolen
Mi hanno rubato la macchina
*mee **an**-noh roo-**bah**-toh la **mak**-kee-na*

My handbag has been stolen
Mi hanno rubato la borsa
*mee **an**-noh roo-**bah**-toh la **bohr**-sa*

22

Common problems

My wallet has been stolen
Mi hanno rubato il portafoglio
*mee **an**-noh roo-**bah**-toh eel pohr-ta-**fo**-lyoh*

My son is lost
Mio figlio si è perduto
***mee**-oh **fee**-lyoh see e payr-**doo**-toh*

Please give me back my passport
Per favore, mi restituisca il passaporto
*payr fa-**voh**-ray, mee ray-stee-too-**ee**-ska eel pas-sa-**por**-toh*

AT THE AIRPORT

Arrival

Here is my passport
Ecco il passaporto
*ek-koh eel pas-sa-**por**-toh*

I am attending a convention
Sono qui per un congresso
*__soh__-noh kwee payr oon kohn-**gres**-soh*

I am here on business
Sono qui in viaggio d'affari
*__soh__-noh kwee een **vyaj**-joh daf-**fah**-ree*

I will be staying here for eight weeks
Starò qui per due mesi
*sta-**ro** kwee payr **doo**-ay **may**-zee*

How much do I have to pay?
Quanto devo pagare?
*__kwan__-toh **day**-voh pa-**gah**-ray*

I have nothing to declare
Non ho niente da dichiarare
*nohn oh **nyen**-tay da dee-kyah-**rah**-ray*

Common problems and requests

I have the usual allowances
Ho le solite cose che si possono portare
*oh lay **so**-lee-tay **co**-zay kay see **pos**-soh-noh pohr-**tah**-ray*

This is for my own use
Questo è per uso personale
***kwe**-stoh e payr **oo**-zoh payr-soh-**nah**-lay*

We are visiting friends
Siamo venuti a trovare degli amici
***syah**-moh vay-**noo**-tee a troh-**vah**-ray **day**-lyee a-**mee**-chee*

We have a joint passport
Abbiamo un passaporto in comune
*ab-**byah**-moh oon pas-sa-**por**-toh een koh-**moo**-nay*

Common problems and requests

Where will I find the airline representative?
Dove posso trovare il responsabile della linea aerea?
***doh**-vay **pos**-soh troh-**vah**-ray eel res-pon-**sa**-bee-lay
  dayl-la **lee**-nay-a a-**ay**-ray-a*

Can I upgrade to first class?
Posso pagare il supplemento prima classe?
***pos**-soh pa-**gah**-ray eel soop-play-**men**-toh **pree**-ma **kla**-say*

Common problems and requests

The people who were to meet me have not arrived
Quelli che dovevano venirmi a prendere non sono arrivati
kwel-lee kay doh-vay-va-noh vay-neer-mee a prayn-day-ray
  nohn soh-noh ar-ree-vah-tee

Where do I get the connection flight to Messina?
Dove prendo il volo di collegamento per Messina?
doh-vay prayn-doh eel voh-loh dee koh-lay-ga-men-to payr
  Mays-see-na

How long will the delay be?
Quanto è il ritardo?
kwan-toh e eel ree-tahr-doh

I am late
Sono in ritardo
soh-noh een ree-tahr-doh

I have lost my ticket
Ho perso il biglietto
oh per-soh eel bee-lyayt-toh

I have missed my connection
Ho perso la coincidenza
oh per-soh la koh-een-chee-dent-sa

Where is the bar?
Dov'è il bar?
doh-ve eel bahr

26

Where is — the departure board (listing)?
  Dov'è — l'orario delle partenze?
  *doh-ve — loh-**rah**-ryoh **day**-lay par-**ten**-tsay*

  — the information desk?
  — il banco informazioni?
  *— eel **ban**-koh een-fohr-ma-**tsyoh**-nee*

  — the lounge?
  — l'atrio dell'albergo?
  *— **la**-tryoh **dayl**-lal-**bayr**-goh*

  — the toilet?
  — la toilette?
  *— la toh-ee layt-ta (twa-**let**)*

  — the transfer desk?
  — il banco per il transfer?
  *— eel **ban**-koh payr eel **trans**-fayr*

Luggage

Can I check in my bags?
Posso fare il check in del mio bagaglio?
***pos**-soh **fah**-ray eel chayk een dayl **mee**-oh ba-**ga**-lyoh*

How much is it per bag?
Quanto si paga per ogni collo?
***kwan**-toh see **pa**-ga payr **oh**-nyee col-loh*

Luggage

I have lost my bag
Ho perso il bagaglio
oh per-soh eel ba-ga-lyoh

It is a large suitcase
E' una valigia grande
e oo-na va-lee-ja gran-day

It is a rucksack
E' uno zaino
e oo-noh tsa-ee-noh

It is a small bag
E' una valigia piccola
e oo-na va-lee-ja peek-koh-la

My baggage has not arrived
Il mio bagaglio non è arrivato
eel mee-oh ba-ga-lyoh nohn e ar-ree-vah-toh

Are there any baggage trolleys?
Ci sono carrelli per i bagagli?
cee soh-noh kar-rel-lee payr ee ba-ga-lyee

Can I have help with my baggage?
Qualcuno mi può aiutare con i bagagli?
kwahl-koo-noh mee pwo a-yoo-tah-ray kohn ee ba-ga-lyee

No, do not put that on top
No, non metta questo sopra il resto
no, nohn mayt-ta kwe-stoh soh-pra eel re-stoh

Careful, the handle is broken
Attenzione, il manico è rotto
*at-tayn-**tsyoh**-nay, eel **ma**-nee-koh e **roht**-toh*

Is there any charge?
Si paga?
*see **pah**-ga*

Please take these bags to a taxi
Per favore, porti questi bagagli fino a un taxi
*payr-fa-**voh**-ray, **pohr**-tee kwe-stee ba-**ga**-lyee **fee**-noh a
  oon tas-**see***

I will carry that myself
Questo lo porto io
***kwe**-stoh loh-**pohr**-toh ee-oh*

These bags are not mine
Queste valigie non sono mie
***kwe**-stay va-**lee**-jay nohn **soh**-noh **mee**-ay*

This package is fragile
Questo pacco è fragile
***kwe**-stoh **pak**-koh e **fra**-jee-lay*

Where do I pick up my bags?
Dove riprendo i bagagli?
***doh**-vay ree-**prayn**-doh ee ba-**ga**-lyee*

Luggage

Where is my bag?
Dov'è la mia borsa?
*doh-ve la **mee**-a **bohr**-sa*

Where is the baggage from flight number…?
Dove sono i bagagli del volo numero…?
*doh-vay **soh**-noh ee ba-**ga**-lyee dayl **voh**-loh **noo**-may-roh…*

AT THE HOTEL

Hotel accommodation

Italy has a very wide range of hotel accommodation. At the luxury end of the market there are sumptuously converted castles, villas and medieval *palazzi*. At the other end of the scale are humble guest houses with few facilities but very reasonable rates and often abundant character. Between the two there are hundreds of family-run hotels of all descriptions, chain hotels, motels – and indistinguishable modern concrete blocks along some stretches of coast.

Hotels are graded from the simple 1-star category to the luxury 5-star. As in Britain, the grading reflects the extent of a hotel's facilities rather than how well it is run.

City hotels run from the simple but characterful to the luxurious international-style. For travellers without expense accounts, the best bets are often *pensioni*. These are roughly the equivalent of guest houses, and used to be classified separately from hotels despite the fact that some of them (particularly in cities) are just as comfortable as 2- or even 3-star hotels. Officially they are now all classified as hotels, but many still make use of their former classifications, i.e. 1- to 3-star *pensioni*.

Hotel accommodation

The facilities of *pensioni* are normally simpler than those of hotels but they are generally friendly, pleasant places to stay, usually offering more Italian atmosphere. In the large cities many occupy two or three floors of medieval *palazzi*. Public rooms are frequently furnished with antiques and paintings: you may even find a frescoed ceiling. The bedrooms can be rather dark though and very noisy if in the centre. If you want to be assured of a good night's sleep, ask for *una camera tranquilla* (a quiet room), which will probably face on to an inner courtyard. *Pensioni* with restaurants may insist that you stay on half-board terms from March to the end of September. This doesn't normally apply in cities, where they rarely have their own restaurants.

Rural hotels

Some country hotels are old villas, set in their own grounds and furnished in traditional style. In the last few years, more and more old castles and hamlets have been restored and converted into hotels (and/or self-catering accommodation). But, on the whole, there is a shortage of small charming hotels in rural regions, such as you find all over France.

Along the coasts, good hotels are hard to find except in the luxury bracket. Large stretches of shoreline have been developed with purpose-built concrete blocks. Where they exist, the older elegant hotels or self-contained luxury hotels are very expensive. In very popular coastal areas in peak season you may be obliged to stay for three nights.

Hotel accommodation

A *locanda* or inn is theoretically the most basic category of accommodation, but some places using this name are just as comfortable as a 2-star hotel and the occasional one is quite fashionable and expensive.

Day hotels
Alberghi diurni or day hotels are a specifically Italian institution, existing in most major towns and usually situated near the main railway station. They can be very useful if you have a long wait for a train, providing bathrooms, hairdressers, cleaning services, rest and reading rooms, but no overnight accommodation. Those in cities such as Florence, Rome and Milan are particularly well equipped. Prices are shown at the entrance and you pay in advance. Opening times are 6am to midnight.

Prices
Charges vary according to class, season and facilities. but every hotel has its fixed rates agreed with the local tourist board. There are very pronounced variations in price between regions – more so than in Britain and perhaps France.

Rome is fairly expensive, but the two most expensive places to stay in Italy are Venice and Capri. Hotels in cities, especially in the main tourist areas, are relatively more expensive than the same quality of accommodation. In rural regions – so you may be able to save by staying at a hotel in the countryside and taking day-trips into the city centre.

If you are considering a package holiday to any Italian

Hotel accommodation

coast it's worth checking before making the booking whether the price includes free beach facilities. Charges made locally for use of deckchairs and umbrellas can often mount up to considerable sums, particularly for a sizeable family.

Booking a hotel

Booking in advance is essential in tourist areas during peak season – particularly in the main cities, where there is simply not enough accommodation to satisfy an ever-increasing demand. From June through to the end of September it is not unusual for rooms in Venice, Florence and Rome to be completely booked up many months ahead. You may get a room if you turn up without a booking, but it's likely to be in the least salubrious part of the city. Outside the peak tourist season, conferences and trade fairs can place similar stresses on local resources at particular times.

Country accommodation is not such a problem, but if you're hoping to stay in some charming little hotel recommended in guidebooks you should certainly reserve well in advance.

On confirmation of a hotel booking, you will normally be required to send a non-returnable deposit. The post to and from Italy is notoriously slow; there is the alternative of a courier service, but it is often simplest to telephone or to send a fax to make the reservation, even if you speak only a little Italian. There is often someone among the hotel staff who speaks English. Travel agents or hotel representatives in this country can make bookings for you, but the latter usually deal only with 4- or 5-star hotels.

Choosing hotels

The Italian Tourist Office in London (1 Princes Street, London W1R 8AY) can provide lists of hotels for most regions. When looking for accommodation on the spot, it's worth trying the local *azienda di soggiorno* (tourist office), which should have details of any rooms vacant in the area.

Hotel chains are not very important in Italy, though they do exist. AGIP and ACI (Automobile Club Italiano) motels are dependable, although impersonal, and very useful for motorists – they are often strategically positioned to fill gaps on the map. Some of the more prominent chains or marketing consortia are at the top end of the market. The Relais et Châteaux and Atahotels groups, for example, are about the most exclusive. Italhotels are comfortable and convenient.

On arrival

On arrival you will be expected to fill in a registration form with your name, address and passport number, and to leave your passport with the receptionist for a while. Make sure you get it back when you go out from the hotel – you're supposed to carry it.

Rates are quoted per room rather than per person, unless you are on half- or full-board terms. Tax and service are nor-

Hotel accommodation

mally included in the room rate. Exceptions are de luxe hotels, which are required to levy a higher rate of VAT and do not usually include this in the quoted price of the room. Another extra to beware of is air-conditioning, often charged per person per night. The price of your room should be posted on the back of your bedroom or bathroom door. If this doesn't tally with the price you have been quoted, check with reception.

Seasonal price differences vary according to the regions. On the coasts and in the lakes, high season is almost invariably July and August, and mid-season rates apply in May, June and September. But in cities lower rates normally apply only in winter.

Breakfast

The typical Italian hotel breakfast consists of coffee, crusty hollow rolls, pre-packed butter and jam. If you are lucky (or staying in quite an expensive hotel), you will get croissants and orange juice too – although it's more likely to be *succo* (tinned or bottled) than *spremuta* (freshly squeezed). Some of the larger hotels offer a full English breakfast.

Breakfast is theoretically an optional extra, and it's usually cheaper and often nicer to take it in a local café. But hotels in Venice, Florence, Rome and other big cities will quote room rates with breakfast included and won't be pleased if you take it elsewhere and demand a reduction on the bill. If you specifically don't want breakfast, say so when you book the room. Other hotels will probably quote breakfast prices separately.

Reservations and enquiries

I have a reservation
Ho prenotato
oh pray-noh-ta-toh

I shall be staying until July 4th
Mi fermo fino al quattro luglio
mee fayr-moh fee-noh al kwat-troh loo-lyoh

I want to stay for 5 nights
Mi fermo cinque notti
mee fayr-moh cheen-kway not-tee

I am sorry I am late
Scusi il ritardo
skoo-zee eel -ree-tahr-doh

I was delayed at the airport
Ho fatto tardi all'aeroporto
oh fat-toh tahr-dee al-la-ay-roh-pohr-toh

I was held up at immigration
L'ufficio immigrazione mi ha fatto fare tardi
loof-fee-choh eem-mee-gra-tsyoh-nay mee a fat-toh fah-ray tahr-dee

37

Reservations and enquiries

How much is it per night?
Quanto costa per notte?
kwan-toh koh-sta payr not-tay

How much is the room per night?
Quanto costa la stanza per notte?
kwan-toh koh-sta la stan-tsa payr not-tay

I need a double room with a bed for a child
Ho bisogno di una stanza matrimoniale con un letto per un
  bambino
*oh bee-zoh-nyoh dee oo-na stan-tsa ma-tree-moh-nya-lay
  kohn oon let-toh payr oon bam-bee-noh*

I need a room with a double bed
Ho bisogno di una stanza matrimoniale
oh bee-zoh-nyoh dee oo-na stan-tsa ma-tree-moh-nya-lay

I need a room with twin beds and bath
Ho bisogno di una stanza con due letti e bagno
*oh bee-zoh-nyoh dee oo-na stan-tsa kohn doo-ay let-tee ay
  ba-nyoh*

I need a single room
Ho bisogno di una stanza singola
oh bee-zoh-nyoh dee oo-na stan-tsa seen-goh-la

I need a single room with a shower or bath
Ho bisogno di una stanza singola con doccia o bagno
*oh bee-zoh-nyoh dee oo-na stan-tsa seen-goh-la kohn
  doh-cha oh ba-nyoh*

Reservations and enquiries

Do you have a single room?
Avete una stanza singola?
*a-vay-tay **oo**-na **stan**-tsa **seen**-goh-la*

Do you have a double room with a bath?
Avete una stanza matrimoniale con bagno?
*a-vay-tay **oo**-na **stan**-tsa ma-tree-moh-**nya**-lay kohn **ba**-nyoh*

Do you have a room with twin beds and a shower?
Avete una stanza con due letti e doccia?
*a-vay-tay **oo**-na-**stan**-tsa kohn **doo**-ay **let**-tee ay **doh**-cha*

Does the price include room and all meals?
Il prezzo comprende stanza e tutti i pasti?
*eel **pret**-tsoh kohm-**pren**-day **stan**-tsa ay **toot**-tee ee pa-stee*

Does the price include room and breakfast?
Il prezzo comprende stanza e colazione?
*eel **pret**-tsoh kohm-**pren**-day **stan**-tsa ay koh-la-**tsyoh**-nay*

Does the price include room and dinner?
Il prezzo comprende stanza e cena?
*eel **pret**-tsoh kohm-**pren**-day **stan**-tsa ay **chay**-na*

How much is — full board?
    Quant'è — la pensione completa?
    *kwan-**te** — la payn-**syoh**-nay kohm-**ple**-ta*

        — half-board?
        — la mezza pensione?
        *— la **med**-za payn-**syoh**-nay*

Reservations and enquiries

Do you take traveller's cheques?
Accettate traveller's cheques?
a-chayt-tah-tay tra-vayl-layrs cheks

Can we have adjoining rooms?
Possiamo avere delle stanze adiacenti?
pos-sya-moh a-vay-ray dayl-lay stan-tsay a-dya-chen-tee

Do you have a car park?
Avete un parcheggio?
a-vay-tay oon par-kej-joh

Do you have a cot for my baby?
Ha una culla per il bambino?
a oo-na kool-la payr eel bam-bee-noh

Is this a safe area?
E' una zona senza pericoli?
e oo-na dzo-na sen-tsa pay-ree-koh-lee

Which floor is my room on?
A che piano è la mia stanza?
a -kay pya-noh e la mee-a stan-tsa

Are there other children staying at the hotel?
Ci sono altri bambini nell'albergo?
chee soh-noh al-tree bam-bee-nee nayl-lal-ber-goh

Are there supervised activities for the children?
Ci sono delle attività sorvegliate per i bambini?
*chee soh-noh dayl-lay at-tee-vee-ta sohr-vay-lya-tay payr
  ee bam-bee-nee*

Reservations and enquiries

Can my son sleep in our room?
Mio figlio può dormire in stanza con noi?
mee-oh fee-lyoh pwo dohr-mee-ray een stan-tsa kohn noh-ee

Do you have a laundry service?
Avete un servizio lavanderia?
a-vay-tay oon sayr-vee-tsyoh la-van-day-ree-a

Is there a room service menu?
C'è un menù per il servizio in camera?
che oon may-noo payr eel sayr-vee-tsyoh een ka-may-ra

When does the bar open?
Quando apre il bar?
kwan-doh ah-pray eel bahr

What time do you close?
A che ora chiudete?
a kay oh-ra kyoo-day-tay

What time does the hotel close?
A che ora chiude l'albergo?
a kay oh-ra kyoo-day lal-bayr-goh

What time does the restaurant close?
A che ora chiude il ristorante?
a kay oh-ra kyoo-day eel ree-stoh-ran-tay

What time is — breakfast?
A che ora c'è — la prima colazione?
a kay oh-ra che— la pree-ma koh-la-tsyo-nay

Reservations and enquiries

— **dinner?**
— la cena?
— *la **chay**-na*

— **lunch?**
— il pranzo?
— *eel **pran**-dzoh*

Is there a market in the town?
C'è un mercato in città?
*che oon mayr-**ka**-toh een cheet-**ta***

Is there a Chinese restaurant?
C'è un ristorante cinese?
*che oon ree-stoh-**ran**-tay chee-**nay**-zay*

Is there an Indian restaurant?
C'è un ristorante indiano?
*che oon ree-stoh-**ran**-tay een-**dyah**-noh*

Is there — a hairdryer?
    C'è — un fon?
    che — oon fon

— **a telephone?**
— un telefono?
— *oon tay-**lay**-foh-noh*

— **a television?**
— una televisione?
— ***oo**-na tay-lay-vee-**zyoh**-nay*

— **a trouser press?**
— uno stiracalzoni?
— *oo-noh stee-ra-kal-tsoh-nee*

— **a lift?**
— un ascensore?
— *oon a-shayn-tsoh-ray*

— **a minibar?**
— un minibar?
— *oon mee-nee-bahr*

— **a sauna?**
— una sauna?
— *oo-na sa-oo-na*

— **a swimming pool?**
— una piscina?
— *oo-na pee-shee-na*

— **a casino?**
— un casinò?
— *oon ka-zee-no*

Is the voltage 220 or 110?
Il voltaggio è duecentoventi o centodieci?
eel vohl-taj-joh e doo-ay-chen-toh-vayn-tee oh chen-toh-dye-chee

Do you have a fax machine?
Avete un fax?
a-vay-tay oon fax

Service

Do you have a safe for valuables?
Avete una cassaforte per i preziosi?
a-vay-tay oo-na kas-sa-for-tay

Do you have any English newspapers?
Avete giornali inglesi?
a-vay-tay johr-nah-lee een-glay-zee

Do you have satellite TV?
Avete la televisione via satellite?
a-vay-tay la tay-lay-vee-zyoh-nay vee-a sa-tel-lee-tay

Service

Can we have breakfast in our room, please?
Per favore, possiamo avere la colazione in camera?
*payr fa-voh-ray, pos-sya-moh a-vay-ray la koh-la-tsyo-nay
  een ka-may-ra*

Can I charge this to my room?
Posso aggiungerlo al conto della stanza?
pos-soh aj-joon-jayr-loh al kohn-toh day-la stan-tsa

Can I have a newspaper?
Posso avere un giornale?
pos-soh a-vay-ray oon johr-nah-lay

Can I have an outside line?
Mi può passare una linea esterna?
mee pwo pas-sah-ray oo-na lee-nay-a ay-ster-na

Can I dial direct from my room?
Posso telefonare direttamente dalla mia stanza?
*pos-soh tay-lay-foh-**nah**-ray **dal**-la **mee**-a **stan**-tsa*

Can I use my personal computer here?
Posso usare il mio computer?
*pos-soh oo-**zah**-ray eel **mee**-oh kohm-**poo**-tayr*

Can I hire a portable telephone?
Posso affittare un telefono portatile?
*pos-soh af-feet-**tah**-ray oon tay-**lay**-foh-noh pohr-**tah**-tee-lay*

Can I make a telephone call from here?
Posso fare una telefonata da qui?
*pos-soh **fah**-ray **oo**-na tay-lay-foh-**na**-ta da kwee*

Can you keep my wallet in the safe?
Potete tenere il mio portafoglio in cassaforte?
*poh-**tay**-tay tay-**nay**-ray eel **mee**-oh pohr-ta-**fo**-lyoh een
cas-sa-**for**-tay*

Can you recommend a good local restaurant?
Mi può consigliare un buon ristorante qui vicino?
*mee pwo kohn-see-**lyah**-ray oon bwohn ree-stoh-**ran**-tay
kwee vee-**chee**-noh*

Can I send this by courier?
Posso mandarlo per corriere?
*pos-soh man-dahr-loh payr-koh-**rye**-ray*

Service

Can I use my charge card?
Posso usare la mia carta di credito?
pos-soh oo-zah-ray la mee-a kar-ta dee kray-dee-toh

Please fill the minibar
Per piacere, riempite il minibar
payr pya-chay-ray, ree aym-pee-tay eel mee-nee-bahr

Please can I leave a message?
Posso lasciare un messaggio?
pos-soh la-shah-ray oon mays-saj-joh

My room number is 22
La mia stanza è la numero ventidue
la mee-a stan-tsa e la noo-may-roh vayn-tee-doo-ay

Has my colleague arrived yet?
E' arrivato il mio collega?
e ar-ree-vah-toh eel mee-oh kohl-lay-ga

I am expecting a fax
Aspetto un fax
a-spet-toh oon fax

Please send this fax for me
Per piacere, mi vuole inviare questo fax
payr pya-chay-ray, mee vwo-lay een-vyah-ray kwe-stoh fax

Please turn the heating off
Per favore, spegnete il riscaldamento
payr-fa-voh-ray, spay-nyay-tay eel ree-skal-da-mayn-toh

What time is it in New York?
Che ora è a New York?
kay oh-ra e a New York

I need an early morning call
Ho bisogno che mi svegliate presto
oh bee-zoh-nyoh kay mee svay-lyah-tay pre-stoh

Please wake me at 7 o'clock in the morning
Per favore, mi svegli alle 7
payr fa-voh-ray, mee svay-lyee al-lay set-tay

I need to make a phone call
Ho bisogno di fare una telefonata
oh bee-zoh-nyoh dee fah-ray oo-na tay-lay-foh-na-ta

Where can I send a fax?
Dove posso mandare un fax?
doh-vay pos-soh man-dah-ray oon fax

Can I have — another blanket?
Mi dà — un'altra coperta?
mee da — oo-nal-tra koh-payr-ta

— another pillow?
— un altro cuscino?
— oo-nal-troh koo-shee-noh

— some coat hangers?
— degli attaccapanni?
— day-lyee at-tac-ca-pan-nee

— **some note paper?**
— della carta da scrivere?
— *day-la kar-ta da skree-vay-ray*

I need — a razor
Ho bisogno — di un rasoio
oh bee-zoh-nyoh — dee oon ra-zoh-yoh

— **some soap**
— di un sapone
— *dee oon sa-poh-nay*

— **some towels**
— di asciugamani
— *dee a-shoo-ga-mah-nee*

Can I have my key, please?
Mi dà la chiave, per piacere?
mee da la kyah-vay payr pya-chay-ray

I need to charge these batteries
Ho bisogno di ricaricare queste batterie
*oh bee-zoh-nyoh dee ree-ka-ree-kah-ray kwe-stay
  bat-tay-ree-ay*

I want to press these clothes
Voglio far stirare questi vestiti
vo-lyoh far stee-rah-ray kwe-stee vay-stee-tee

Problems

Can I speak to the manager?
Posso parlare con il direttore?
pos-soh par-lah-ray kohn eel dee-rayt-toh-ray

Where is the manager?
Dov'è il direttore?
doh-ve eel dee-rayt-toh-ray

I cannot close the window
Non riesco a chiudere la finestra
nohn ree-e-skoh a kyoo-day-ray la fee-ne-stra

I cannot open the window
Non riesco ad aprire la finestra
nohn ree-e-skoh ad a-pree-ray la fee-ne-stra

I need some toilet paper
Ho bisogno di carta igienica
oh bee-zoh-nyoh dee kar-ta ee-jay-nee-ka

The air conditioning is not working
L'aria condizionata non funziona
la-rya kohn-dee-tsyo-nah-ta nohn foon-tsyoh-na

The bathroom is dirty
Il bagno è sporco
eel ba-nyoh e spor-koh

Problems

The heating is not working
Il riscaldamento non funziona
*eel ree-skal-da-**mayn**-toh nohn foon-**tsyoh**-na*

The light is not working
La luce non funziona
*la **loo**-chay nohn foon-**tsyoh**-na*

The room is not serviced
La stanza non viene pulita
*la **stan**-tsa nohn **vyay**-nay poo-**lee**-ta*

The room is too noisy
La stanza è troppo rumorosa
*la **stan**-tsa e **trop**-poh roo-moh-**roh**-za*

The room key does not work
La chiave della stanza non funziona
*la **kyah**-vay **dayl**-la **stan**-tsa nohn foon-**tsyoh**-na*

There are no towels in the room
In camera non ci sono asciugamani
*een **ka**-may-ra nohn chee **soh**-noh a-shoo-ga-**mah**-nee*

There is no hot water
Non c'è acqua calda
*nohn che **ak**-kwa **kal**-da*

There is no plug for the washbasin
Non c'è il tappo nel lavandino
*nohn che eel **tap**-poh nayl la-van-**dee**-noh*

Checking out

I have to leave tomorrow
Parto domani
*pahr-toh doh-**mah**-nee*

I want to stay an extra night
Voglio fermarmi un'altra notte
*vo-lyoh fayr-**mahr**-mee oo-**nal**-tra **not**-tay*

Do I have to change rooms?
Devo cambiare stanza?
***day**-voh kam-**byah**-ray **stan**-tsa*

We will be leaving early tomorrow
Partiamo domani mattina presto
*par-**tyah**-moh doh-**mah**-nee mat-**tee**-na*

Could you have my bags brought down?
Mi potreste portare giù i bagagli?
*mee poh-**tray**-stay pohr-**tah**-ray joo ee ba-**ga**-lyee*

Please leave the bags in the lobby
Per piacere, lasci i bagagli nell'atrio
*payr pya-**chay**-ray, **la**-shee ee ba-**ga**-lyee nayl-**la**-tree-oh*

Could you order me a taxi?
Mi può chiamare un taxi?
*mee pwo kya-**mah**-ray oon tas-**see***

Checking out

Can I have the bill please?
Posso avere il conto, per favore?
pos-soh a-**vay**-ray eel **kohn**-toh, payr fa-**voh**-ray

Thank you, we enjoyed our stay
Grazie, è stato un ottimo soggiorno
gra-tsyay, e **stah**-toh oon **ot**-tee-moh sohj-**johr**-noh

OTHER ACCOMMODATION

Self-catering

Self-catering holidays in Italy are becoming more and more popular, and the choice of accommodation has greatly expanded over the last few years with the development of *Agriturismo*, a scheme whereby barns and other farm buildings are converted and let out to tourists. Now you can stay in country cottages, farmhouses, old villas, mills, studio flats, villas on the sea, modern apartments or tourist villages complete with their own shops, restaurants and sports facilities.

Where to go

Two of the most popular self-catering areas for British visitors are Tuscany and Umbria. These regions offer a whole range of delightful rural properties, many of them in the hills and villages around the main historic towns. The properties range from small cottages to large luxury villas with pools, and there are even castles in country estates. Along the Tuscan coast most of the self-catering accommodation is in simple villas.

Along the popular coastlines of Italy, particularly the Rivi-

Renting a house

era and the Adriatic, the accommodation is mainly in high-rise apartment blocks, often with the use of communal pool, restaurant and shops. Prices are quite reasonable but the units can be rather plain and functional.

Tourist villages, consisting of self-catering villas or apartments, tend to be in or near the main resorts. Sardinia and Sicily are both popular for self-catering holidays and offer accommodation in apartments, villas and holiday villages.

Finding accommodation
An increasing number of tour operators offer self-catering package holidays in Italy. You can choose either a ferry package, based on taking your own car, or an air package, with or without hired car. (If you are staying in a country area, you will probably find life without a car difficult.) There are also numerous properties for rent on an accommodation-only basis through agencies. To make your own arrangements, write to the tourist office of the region you're planning to visit for a list of properties or to Agriturist, Corso V. Emanuele 101, Rome 00168.

Renting a house

We have rented this villa
Abbiamo affittato questa villa
ab-**byah**-moh af-*feet*-**ta**-toh **kwe**-sta **veel**-la

Renting a house

Here is our booking form
Ecco il modulo di prenotazione
ek-koh eel mo-doo-loh dee pray-noh-ta-tsyoh-nay

We need two sets of keys
Abbiamo bisogno di due paia di chiavi
ab-byah-moh bee-zoh-nyoh dee doo-ay pa-ya dee kyah-vee

When does the cleaner come?
Quando viene la donna delle pulizie?
kwan-doh vyay-nay la don-na dayl-lay poo-lee-tsee-ay

Can I contact you on this number?
La posso contattare a questo numero?
la pos-soh kohn-tat-tah-ray a kwe-stoh noo-may-roh

How does this work?
Questo come funziona?
kwe-stoh koh-may foon-tsyoh-na

Where is the bathroom?
Dov'è il bagno?
doh-ve eel ba-nyoh

What is the voltage here?
Qual'è il voltaggio qui?
kwah-le eel vohl-taj-joh kwee

I cannot open the shutters
Non riesco ad aprire le imposte
nohn ree-e-skoh ad a-pree-ray lay eem-po-stay

Renting a house

Is the water heater working?
Funziona il boiler?
*foon-**tsyoh**-na eel **boh**-ee-layr*

Is the water safe to drink?
L'acqua è potabile?
***lak**-kwa e poh-**ta**-bee-lay*

Is there any spare bedding?
C'è dell'altra biancheria?
*che dayl-**lal**-tra byan-kay-**ree**-a*

The cooker does not work
I fornelli non funzionano
*ee fohr-**nel**-lee nohn foon-**tsyoh**-na-noh*

The refrigerator does not work
Il frigo non funziona
*eel **free**-goh nohn foon-**tsyoh**-na*

The toilet is blocked
Il gabinetto è otturato
*eel ga-bee-**nayt**-toh e ot-too-**ra**-toh*

There is a leak
C'è una perdita
*che **oo**-na **per**-dee-ta*

We do not have any water
Non abbiamo acqua
*nohn ab-**byah**-moh **ak**-kwa*

Can you send a plumber?
Potete mandare un idraulico?
*poh-**tay**-tay man-**dah**-ray oon ee-**dra**-oo-lee-koh*

Where is the fuse box?
Dove sono i fusibili?
*doh-vay **soh**-noh ee foo-**see**-bee-lee*

Where is the key for this door?
Dov'è la chiave di questa porta?
*doh-**ve** la **kyah**-vay dee **kwe**-sta **por**-ta*

Where is the socket for my razor?
Dov'è l'attacco per il rasoio elettrico?
*doh-**ve** lat-**tak**-koh payr eel ra-**zo**-yoh ay-**let**-tree-koh*

Around the house

bath
bagno
***ba**-nyoh*

washbasin
lavandino
*la-van-**dee**-noh*

toilet
gabinetto
*ga-bee-**nayt**-toh*

bathroom
bagno
***ba**-nyoh*

vacuum cleaner
aspirapolvere
*a-**spee**-ra-**pohl**-vay-ray*

bed
letto
***let**-toh*

Around the house

brush
spazzola
spats-soh-la

tap
rubinetto
roo-bee-nayt-toh

kitchen
cucina
koo-chee-na

knife
coltello
kohl-tel-loh

mirror
specchio
spek-kyoh

pan
pentola
payn-toh-la

plate
piatto
pyat-toh

refrigerator
frigorifero
free-goh-ree-fay-roh

sheet
lenzuolo
layn-tswo-loh

sink
lavello
la-vel-loh

spoon
cucchiaio
kook-kya-ee-yoh

stove
stufa
stoo-fa

table
tavola
ta-voh-la

can opener
apriscatole
a-pree-ska-toh-lay

chair
sedia
se-dya

cooker
fornelli
fohr-nel-lee

corkscrew
cavatappi
ka-va-tap-pee

fork
forchetta
fohr-kayt-ta

cup
tazza
tats-sa

glass
bicchiere
beek-kye-ray

Camping

There are over 1,600 camp sites in Italy, with the main concentration along coasts and lake shores. Many of the sites are attractively located, often in wooded areas, but, on the whole, standards and facilities are lower than those of sites in Austria, Switzerland or Germany, for example.

One of the main problems is overcrowding in high season, particularly near the sea, where sites tend to squeeze in as many tents and caravans as possible.

There is no official grading system, and the tariffs vary widely according to the area and the type of site. Not surprisingly, more facilities generally means more expensive.

You can get full details of camp sites from the annual publication *Campeggi e Villaggi Turistici in Italia,* published by the Touring Club Italiano and Federcampeggio, available in Italian bookshops. A shorter list of sites (with a map) is available from the Italian Tourist Office, 1 Princes Street, London W1R 8AY.

On the camp site

Many sites, especially those near large cities, are open all year. If you're going in high season it's advisable to book in advance.

Off-site camping is not allowed, wihout the permission of the owner of the property.

On the camp site

Can we camp in your field?
Possiamo montare la tenda nel suo campo?
pos-syah-moh mon-ta-ray la ten-da nayl soo-oh kam-poh

Can we camp near here?
Possiamo montare la tenda qui vicino?
pos-syah-moh mon-ta-ray la ten-da kwee vee-chee-noh

Can we park our caravan here?
Possiamo parcheggiare qui la nostra roulotte?
pos-syah-moh par-kayj-jah-ray kwee la nos-tra roo-lot

Do I pay in advance?
Devo pagare prima?
day-voh pa-gah-ray pree-ma

Do I pay when I leave?
Pago quando parto?
pah-goh kwan-doh par-toh

On the camp site

Is there a more sheltered site ?
C'è un posto più riparato?
*che oon **poh**-stoh pyoo ree-pa-**rah**-toh*

Is there a restaurant or a shop on the site?
C'è un ristorante o un negozio nel campeggio?
*che oon ree-stoh-**ran**-tay oh oon nay-**go**-tsyo nayl kam-**payj**-joh*

Is there another campsite near there?
C'è un campeggio qui vicino?
*che oon kam-**payj**-joh kwee vee-**chee**-noh*

Is this the drinking water?
Quest'acqua è potabile?
*kwe-**stak**-kwa e poh-**ta**-bee-lay*

Please can we pitch our tent here?
Per piacere, possiamo montare la tenda qui?
*payr pya-**chay**-ray, pos-**syah**-moh mon-**ta**-ray la **ten**-da kwee*

The site is very wet and muddy
Il campeggio è molto bagnato e pieno di fango
*eel kam-**payj**-joh e **mohl**-toh ba-**nyah**-toh ay **pye**-noh dee **fan**-goh*

Where are the toilets?
Dove sono le toilette?
*doh-vay **soh**-noh lay toh-ee-**layt**-tay (...twa-**let**)*

61

Around the camp site

Where can I have a shower?
Dove posso fare la doccia?
*doh-vay **pos**-soh **fah**-ray la **doh**-cha*

Where can we wash our dishes?
Dove possiamo lavare i piatti?
*doh-vay pos-**syah**-moh la-**va**-ray ee **pyat**-tee*

Around the camp site

air mattress
materassino ad aria
*ma-tay-ras-**see**-noh ad **ah**-rya*

backpack
zaino
dza-ee-noh

bottle-opener
apribottiglia
*a-pree-boht-**tee**-lya*

bucket
secchio
sayk-kyoh

camp bed
lettino da campo
*let-**tee**-noh da **kam**-poh*

camp chair
sedia da campo
*se-dya da **kam**-poh*

can-opener
apriscatole
*a-pree-**ska**-toh-lay*

candle
candela
*kan-**day**-la*

cup
tazza
tats-sa

fire
fuoco
fwo-koh

Around the camp site

flashlight
pila
pee-la

fly sheet
sopratetto della tenda
soh-pra-tayt-toh day-la ten-da

folding table
tavola pieghevole
ta-voh-la pyay-gay-voh-lay

fork
forchetta
fohr-kayt-ta

frying pan
padella
pa-del-la

ground sheet
catino
ca-tee-noh

ground
terra
ter-ra

guy line
corda
kor-da

knife
coltello
kohl-tel-loh

mallet
martello di legno
mar-tel-loh dee lay-nyoh

matches
fiammiferi
fyam-mee-fay-ree

pail
secchio
sayk-kyoh

penknife
temperino
taym-pay-ree-noh

plate
piatto
pyat-toh

rucksack
zaino
dza-ee-noh

shelter
riparo
ree-pah-roh

Hostelling

sleeping bag	**tent pole**
sacco a pelo	bastone
*sak-koh a **pay**-loh*	*ba-**stoh**-nay*
spoon	**tent**
cucchiaio	tenda
*kook-**kya**-yoh*	***ten**-da*
stove	**thermos flask**
fornello	termos
*fohr-**nel**-lo*	***tayr**-mohs*
tent peg	**torch**
picchetto	pila
*peek-**kayt**-toh*	***pee**-la*

Hostelling

Most of Italy's hostels belong to the Associazione Italiana Alberghi per la Gioventù (Via Cavour 44, 00184 Roma, Italy) and are listed in the annual directory published by Hostelling International. Rates vary depending on the season and whether you are under 26. You do not always need a Hostelling International membership card, but may have to pay more without one. Hostels are very popular in the summer so advance booking is necessary.

Is there a youth hostel near here?
C'è un ostello qui vicino?
*che oon oh-**stel**-loh kwee vee-**chee**-noh*

Are you open during the day?
Siete aperti durante il giorno?
*syay-tay a-**per**-tee doo-**ran**-tay eel **johr**-noh*

Can we stay five nights here?
Possiamo fermarci qui cinque notti?
*pos-**syah**-moh fayr-**mahr**-chee kwee **cheen**-kway **not**-tee*

Can we stay until Sunday?
Possiamo fermarci fino a domenica?
*pos-**syah**-moh fayr-**mahr**-chee **fee**-noh a doh-**may**-nee-ka*

Here is my membership card
Ecco la tessera di socio
***ek**-koh la **tes**-say-ra dee **soh**-choh*

I do not have my card
Non ho la tessera
*nohn oh la **tes**-say-ra*

Can I join here?
Posso iscrivermi qui?
***pos**-soh ee-**skree**-vayr-mee kwee*

Can I use the kitchen?
Posso usare la cucina?
***pos**-soh oo-**zah**-ray la koo-**chee**-na*

Do you serve meals?
Servite i pasti?
*sayr-**vee**-tay ee **pas**-tee*

Childcare

— to take away?
— da portar via?
— *da pohr-tar vee-a*

What time do you close?
A che ora chiudete?
a kay oh-ra kyoo-day-tay

Childcare

Can you warm this milk for me?
Mi potete riscaldare questo latte?
mee poh-tay-tay ree-skal-dah-ray kwe-stoh lat-tay

Where can I change the baby?
Dove posso cambiare il bambino?
doh-vay pos-soh kam-byah-ray eel bam-bee-noh

Where can I feed my baby?
Dove posso dar da mangiare al bambino?
doh-vay pos-soh dar da man-jahr-ray al bam-bee-noh

Do you have a high chair?
Avete un seggiolone?
a-vay-tay oon sayj-joh-loh-nay

Is there a cot for our baby?
Avete una culla per il bambino?
a-vay-tay oo-na kool-la payr eel bam-bee-noh

Childcare

Is there — a paddling pool?
    C'è — una piscina per i più piccoli?
    che — oo-na pee-shee-na payr ee pyoo peek-koh-lee

        — a swimming pool?
        — una piscina?
        — oo-na pee-shee-na

        — a swing park?
        — un'altalena?
        — oo-nal-ta-lay-na

How old is your daughter?
Quanti anni ha sua figlia?
kwan-tee an-nee a soo-a fee-lya

My daughter is 7 years old
Mia figlia ha sette anni
mee-a fee-lya a set-tay an-nee

My son is 10 years old
Mio figlio ha dieci anni
mee-oh fee-lyoh a dye-chee an-nee

I am very sorry. That was very naughty of him
Mi scusi. Si è comportato malissimo
mee skoo-zee. see e kohm-pohr-ta-toh ma-lees-see-moh

It will not happen again
Non succederà più
nohn soo-chay-day-ra pyoo

Childcare

Is there a baby-sitter?
C'è una baby-sitter?
che oo-na bay-bee-seet-tayr

She goes to bed at nine o'clock
Lei va a letto alle nove
lay-ee va a let-toh al-lay no-vay

We will be back in two hours
Torniamo tra due ore
tohr-nya-moh tra doo-ay oh-ray

Where can I buy some disposable nappies?
Dove posso comprare dei pannolini?
doh-vay pos-soh kohm-prah-ray day-ee pan-noh-lee-nee

GETTING AROUND

Opening hours

Offices, shops banks and some museums generally close at lunchtime. The break tends to be longer in the south and in summer. In some tourist area, shops may stay open all day.

Asking for directions

Where is — the art gallery?
   Dov'é — la galleria d'arte?
   doh-ve — la gal-lay-ree-a dahr-tay

— the post office?
   — l'ufficio postale?
   — *loof-fee-choh poh-stah-lay*

— the Tourist Information Service?
   — l'Ufficio Turistico?
   — *loof-fee-choh too-ree-stee-koh*

Can you show me on the map?
Me lo può mostrare sulla carta?
may loh pwo moh-strah-ray sool-la kar-ta

Asking for directions

Can you tell me the way to the bus station?
Mi può indicare la strada per la stazione dei pullman?
*mee pwo een-dee-**kah**-ray la **strah**-da payr la sta-**tsyoh**-nay*
  *day-ee **pool**-man*

I am lost
Mi sono perduto
*mee **soh**-noh payr-**doo**-toh*

I am lost. How do I get to the Excelsior Hotel?
Mi sono perso. Come arrivo all'Hotel Excelsior?
*mee **soh**-noh **per**-soh. **koh**-may ar-**ree**-voh al-loh-**tayl***
  *eks-**chayl**-syohr*

Can you walk there?
Ci si arriva a piedi?
*chee see ar-**ree**-va a **pye**-dee*

I am looking for the Tourist Information Office
Cerco l'Ufficio Turistico
*chayr-koh loof-fee-choh too-**ree**-stee-koh*

I am trying to get to the market
Sto cercando di arrivare al mercato
*stoh chayr-**kan**-doh dee ar-ree-**vah**-ray al mayr-**kah**-toh*

I want to go to the theatre
Voglio andare a teatro
***vo**-lyoh an-**dah**-ray a tay-**ah**-troh*

Is it far?
E' lontano?
*e lohn-**tah**-noh*

Is there a bus that goes there?
Ci si arriva in pullman?
*chee see ar-**ree**-va een **pool**-man*

Is this the right way to the supermarket?
E' la strada giusta per il supermercato?
*e la **stra**-da **joo**-sta payr eel soo-payr-mayr-**kah**-toh*

We are looking for a restaurant
Cerchiamo un ristorante
*chayr-**kya**-moh oon ree-stoh-**ran**-tay*

Where are the toilets?
Dove sono le toilette?
***doh**-vay **soh**-noh lay toh-ee-**let**-tay (twa-**let**)*

Where do I get a bus for the city centre?
Dove prendo il pullman per il centro?
***doh**-vay **pren**-doh eel **pool**-man payr eel **chen**-troh*

Where do I get the bus for the airport?
Dove prendo il pullman per l'aeroporto?
***doh**-vay **pren**-doh eel **pool**-man payr la-ay-roh-**por**-toh*

Is there a train that goes there?
Ci si arriva in treno?
*chee see ar-**ree**-va een **tre**-noh*

By road

How long does it take to get to the park?
Quanto ci si mette ad arrivare al parco?
*kwan-toh chee see **mayt**-tay ad ar-ree-**vah**-ray al **par**-koh*

By road

Do I turn here for...?
Giro qui per ...?
jee-roh kwee payr...

How do I get onto the motorway?
Come arrivo all'autostrada?
*koh-may ar-**ree**-voh al-la-oo-toh-**strah**-da*

How far is it to Urbino?
Quanto è lontana Urbino?
*kwan-toh e lohn-**tah**-na oor-**bee**-noh*

How long will it take to get there?
Quanto ci vorrà per arrivarci?
*kwan-toh chee vohr-**ra** payr ar-ree-**vahr**-chee*

I am looking for the next exit
Cerco l'uscita più vicina
*chayr-koh loo-**shee**-ta pyoo vee-**chee**-na*

Is there a filling station near here?
C'è un distributore qui vicino?
*che oon dee-stree-boo-**toh**-ray kwee vee-**chee**-noh*

Where does this road go to?
Dove porta questa strada?
doh-vay **pohr**-ta **kwe**-sta **strah**-da

Which is the best route to Bolzano?
Qual è la strada migliore per Bolzano?
kwa-**le** la **stra**-da mee-**lyoh**-ray payr bohl-**tsa**-noh

Which is the fastest route?
Qual è la strada più veloce?
kwa-**le** la **strah**-da pyoo vay-**loh**-chay

Which road do I take to Perugia?
Che strada prendo per Perugia?
kay **strah**-da **pren**-doh payr pay-**roo**-ja

Directions — what you may hear

  Vada — a sinistra
vah-da — *a see-**nee**-stra*
You go — left

> **— a destra**
> — *a de-stra*
> — right

> **— verso . . .**
> — ***ver**-soh . . .*
> — towards . . .

73

Directions — what you may hear

> **— fino a . . .**
> *— fee-noh a . . .*
> — as far as . . .

> **— sotto il ponte**
> *— sot-toh eel **pohn**-tay*
> — under the bridge

Giri a sinistra
*jee-ree a see-**nee**-stra*
Turn left

Giri a destra
*jee-ree a **de**-stra*
Turn right

Vada sempre dritto
*vah-da **sem**-pray **dreet**-toh*
Keep going straight ahead

Segua le indicazioni per la piazza
*say-gwa lay in-dee-**cats**-ee-oh-nee payr la **pyats**-sa*
Follow the signs for the square

Segua le indicazioni per la prossima uscita
*say-gwa lay in-dee-**cats**-ee-oh-nee payr la **pros**-see-ma
  oo-**shee**-ta*
Follow the signs for the next junction

Segua le indicazioni per l'autostrada
*say-gwa lay in-dee-**cats**-ee-oh-nee payr la-oo-toh-**strah**-da*
Follow the signs for the motorway

Directions — what you may hear

E'— all'incrocio
e — al-leen-kroh-choh
It is — at the intersection

— dopo i semafori
— doh-poh ee say-ma-foh-ree
— after the traffic lights

— dietro l'angolo
— dye-troh lan-goh-loh
— around the corner

— accanto al cinema
— ak-kan-toh al chee-nay-ma
— next to the cinema

— al prossimo piano
— al pros-see-moh pyah-noh
— on the next floor

— di fronte alla stazione
— dee frohn-tay al-la sta-tsyoh-nay
— opposite the railway station

— là in fondo
— la een fohn-doh
— over there

Deve tornare indietro
day-vay tohr-nah-ray een-dye-troh
You have to go back

Hiring a car

Attraversi la strada
at-tra-vayr-see la strah-da
Cross the street

Prenda la prima strada a destra
pren-da la pree-ma strah-da a de-stra
Take the first road on the right

Prenda la strada per Chioggia
pren-da la strah-da payr kyoj-ja
Take the road for Chioggia

Prenda la seconda strada a sinistra
pren-da la say-kohn-da strah-da a see-nee-stra
Take the second road on the left

Hiring a car

Car hire is available in most cities and resorts through international and Italian firms. In general, small local firms offer the cheapest rates, but with the major companies you can collect a car from one office and leave it at another for no extra cost.

Can I hire a car?
Posso affittare una macchina?
pos-soh af-feet-tah-ray oo-na mak-kee-na

I want to hire a car
Voglio affittare una macchina
vo-lyoh af-feet-tah-ray oo-na mak-kee-na

I need it for 2 weeks
Ne ho bisogno per due settimane
*nay oh bee-**zoh**-nyoh payr **doo**-ay sayt-tee-**mah**-nay*

Can I hire a car with an automatic gearbox?
Posso affittare una macchina con il cambio automatico?
***pos**-soh af-feet-**tah**-ray **oo**-na **mak**-kee-na kohn eel
kam-byoh a-oo-toh-**ma**-tee-koh*

Do you have — a large car?
      Avete — una macchina grande?
   *a-**vay**-tay — **oo**-na **mak**-kee-na **gran**-day*

        — an automatic?
        — un'automatica?
        *— oo-na-oo-toh-**ma**-tee-ka*

        — an estate car?
        — una giardiniera?
        *— **oo**-na jar-dee-**nye**-ra*

        — a smaller car?
        — una macchina più piccola?
        *— **oo**-na **mak**-kee-na pyoo **peek**-koh-la*

I would like a spare set of keys
Vorrei un altro paio di chiavi
*vor-**re**-ee oon **al**-troh **pa**-yoh dee **kyah**-vee*

Hiring a car

We will both be driving
Guidiamo tutt'e due
*gwee-**dyah**-moh **toot**-tay **doo**-ay*

Can I pay for insurance?
Posso pagare l'assicurazione?
***pos**-soh pa-**gah**-ray las-see-koo-ra-**tsyoh**-nay*

I want to leave a car at the airport
Voglio lasciare la macchina all'aeroporto
***vo**-lyoh la-**shah**-ray la **mak**-kee-na al-la-ay-roh-**por**-toh*

I would like to leave the car at the airport
Vorrei lasciare la macchina all'aeroporto
***vor**-**re**-ee la-**shah**-ray la **mak**-kee-na al-la-ay-roh-**por**-toh*

Is there a charge per kilometre?
C'è un sovraprezzo per chilometro?
*che oon soh-vra-**prets**-soh payr kee-lo-**may**-troh*

Must I return the car here?
Devo riportare qui la macchina?
***day**-voh ree-pohr-**tah**-ray kwee la **mak**-kee-na*

Please explain the documents
Mi spieghi i documenti, per favore
*mee **spyay**-ghee ee doh-koo-**mayn**-tee, payr fa-**voh**-ray*

Please show me how to operate the lights
Mi mostri come si accendono le luci, per favore
*mee **moh**-stree **koh**-may see a-**chen**-doh-noh lay **loo**-chee,
payr fa-**voh**-ray*

Please show me how to operate the windscreen wipers
Mi mostri come far funzioare il tergicristallo, per favore
*mee **moh**-stree **koh**-may fahr foon-tsyoh-**nay**-ray eel
tayr-jee-kree-**stal**-loh, payr fa-**voh**-ray*

How does the steering lock work?
Come funziona il blocca sterzo?
***koh**-may foon-**tsyoh**-na eel **blohk**-ka **ster**-tsoh*

Where is reverse gear?
Dov'è la marcia indietro?
*doh-**ve** la **mar**-cha een-**dye**-troh*

Where is the tool kit?
Dov'è la scatola degli attrezzi?
*doh-**ve** la **skah**-toh-la **day**-lyee at-**trayts**-see*

By taxi

Taxis are available in main towns and tourist resorts. They
are yellow or white and are hired from ranks – not flagged
down in the street. Make sure the meter is used for local city
trips, and if going a long distance agree the price before you
set off. A small tip is expected – 5 per cent of the fare, say.

Where can I get a taxi?
Dove posso trovare un taxi?
doh**-vay **pos**-soh troh-**vah**-ray oon tas-**see

By taxi

Please show us around the town
Per piacere, ci porti a fare un giro per la città
*payr pya-**chay**-ray, chee **pohr**-tee a **fah**-ray oon **jee**-roh
payr la cheet-**ta***

Please take me to this address
Per piacere, mi porti a questo indirizzo
*payr pya-**chay**-ray, mee **pohr**-tee a **kwe**-stoh een-dee-**reets**-soh*

Will you put the bags in the boot?
Può mettere le borse nel bagagliaio?
*pwo **mayt**-tay-ray lay **bohr**-say nayl ba-ga-**lya**-yoh*

Take me to the airport, please
Per favore, mi porti all'aeroporto
*payr fa-**voh**-ray, mee **pohr**-tee al-la-ay-roh-**por**-toh*

The bus station, please
La stazione dei pullman, per favore
*la sta-**tsyoh**-nay **day**-ee **pool**-man, payr fa-**voh**-ray*

Please wait here for a few minutes
Per piacere, aspetti qui per qualche minuto
*payr pya-**chay**-ray, a-**spayt**-tee kwee payr **kwal**-kay
mee-**noo**-toh*

Turn left, please
Giri a sinistra, per favore
*jee-ree a see-**nee**-stra, payr fa-**voh**-ray*

Turn right, please
Giri a destra, per piacere
jee-ree a de-stra, payr pya-chay-ray

Please, stop at the corner
Per piacere, si fermi all'angolo
payr pya-chay-ray, see fayr-mee al-lan-goh-loh

Wait for me please
Mi aspetti, per piacere
mee a-spayt-tee, payr pya-chay-ray

Can you come back in one hour?
Può ritornare tra un'ora?
pwo ree-tohr-nah-ray tra oo-noh-ra

How much is it per kilometre?
Quanto costa al chilometro?
kwan-toh koh-sta al kee-lo-may-troh

Please hurry, I am late
Per piacere, faccia in fretta, sono in ritardo
payr pya-chay-ray, fa-cha een frayt-ta, soh-noh een reetar-doh

How much is that, please?
Quant'è, per piacere?
kwan-te, payr pya-chay-ray

Keep the change
Tenga il resto
tayn-ga eel re-stoh

By bus

Buses are used chiefly for local journeys or in cities. But there are long-distance bus services operated in summer by larger companies, for example SITA. All the main cities (except Venice) provide coach city tours which usually last half a day. It's a good way of getting your bearings if you haven't got a lot of time to explore on foot. Town buses run in the larger cities, with a set price per journey. Monthly season tickets are available.

Does this bus go to the castle?
Questo pullman va al castello?
*kwe-stoh **pool**-man va al ka-**stel**-lo*

How frequent is the service?
Che frequenza ha il servizio?
*kay fray-**kwen**-tsa a eel sayr-**vee**-tsyoh*

Is there a bus into town?
C'è un bus per la città?
*che oon boos payr la cheet-**ta***

What is the fare to the city centre?
Quanto costa il biglietto per il centro?
*kwan-toh **koh**-sta eel beel-**yayt** toh payr eel **chen**-troh*

When is the last bus?
Quando parte l'ultimo pullman?
*kwan-doh **pahr**-tay **lool**-tee-moh **pool**-man*

Where should I change?
Dove devo cambiare?
doh-vay day-voh kam-byah-ray

Which bus do I take for the football stadium?
Che pullman prendo per lo stadio?
kay pool-man prayn-doh payr loh stah-dyoh

Will you tell me when to get off the bus?
Mi dice dove devo scendere?
mee dee-chay doh-vay day-voh shayn-day-ray

By train

For most visitors to Italy, public transport (except in cities, where buses and taxis come into play) means the railway. The network is extensive – even in regions where good roads are few and far between – and fares are low.

Within Italy there are five types of train:
- ETR 450 'Pendolino' – luxury first-class-only trains running between the main cities. A special supplement is charged and a seat reservation is obligatory.
- Intercity – fast trains running between main towns. Some are all first-class coaches. A supplement of roughly 30 per cent of the normal fare is charged.
- Espresso – long-distance trains stopping at main stations.
- Diretto – trains stopping at most stations.
- Locale – local trains stopping at all stations.

There are also Eurocity trains linking Rome and the major

By train

Italian cities with Switzerland, France, Austria and Germany.
   Italian trains get very crowded, particularly in summer,
and seat reservations are recommended; in some Rapido
trains, reservations are obligatory. On overnight trains sleep-
ers and couchettes are available.

Can I buy a return ticket?
Posso fare un biglietto di andata e ritorno?
pos-soh fah-ray oon bee-lyayt-toh dee an-dah-ta ay
  ree-tohr-noh

A return to Milan, please
Un biglietto di andata e ritorno per Milano, per favore
oon bee-lyayt-toh dee an-dah-ta ay ree tohr-noh payr
  mee-lah-noh, payr fa-voh-ray

A return to Paris, first class
Un'andata e ritorno per Parigi, prima classe
oo-nan-dah-ta ay ree-tohr-noh payr pa-ree-jee, pree-ma
  klas-say

A single to Vienna, please
Un biglietto di sola andata per Vienna, per piacere
oon bee-lyayt-to dee soh-la an-dah-ta payr vyen-na, payr
  pya-chay ray

Second class. A window seat, please
Seconda classe, un posto vicino al finestrino, per piacere
say-kohn-da klas-say, oon poh-stoh vee-chee-noh al
  fee-nay-stree-noh, payr pya-chay-ray

A smoking compartment, first-class
Uno scompartimento per fumatori, prima classe
*oo-noh skohm-par-tee-**mayn**-toh payr foo-ma-**toh**-ree,*
* **pree**-ma **klas**-say*

A non-smoking compartment, please
Uno scompartimento per non fumatori, per favore
*oo-noh skohm-par-tee-**mayn**-toh payr nohn foo-ma-**toh**-ree,*
* payr fa-**voh**-ray*

I want to book a seat on the Sleeper to Paris
Voglio prenotare un posto nel vagone letto per Parigi
***vo**-lyoh pray-noh-**tah**-ray oon **poh**-stoh nayl va-**goh**-nay*
* **let**-toh payr pa-**ree**-jee*

What are the times of the trains to Paris?
Qual'è l'orario dei treni per Parigi?
*kwa-**le** loh-**rah**-ryoh **day**-ee **tre**-nee payr pa-**ree**-jee*

What time does the train leave?
A che ora parte il treno?
*a kay **oh**-ra **par**-tay eel **tre**-noh*

What time is the last train?
A che ora parte l'ultimo treno?
*a kay **oh**-ra **par**-tay **lool**-tee-moh **tre**-noh*

When is the next train to Turin?
Quando parte il prossimo treno per Torino?
***kwan**-doh **par**-tay eel **pros**-see-moh **tre**-noh payr to-**ree**-noh*

By train

Where can I buy a ticket?
Dove posso comprare il biglietto?
*doh-vay **pos**-soh kohm-**prah**-ray eel bee-**lyayt**-toh*

Where do I have to change?
Dove devo cambiare?
*doh-vay **day**-voh kam-**byah**-ray*

Which platform do I go to?
A che binario vado?
*a kay -bee-**nah**-ryoh **vah**-doh*

Can I take my bicycle?
Posso portarmi la bicicletta?
*pos-soh pohr-**tar**-mee la bee-chee-**klayt**-ta*

Is there any charge?
Si paga?
*see **pah**-ga*

How long do I have before my next train leaves?
Tra quanto parte il prossimo treno?
*tra **kwan**-toh **par**-tay eel **pros**-see-moh **tre**-noh*

Do I have time to go shopping?
Ho tempo per fare acquisti?
*oh **tem**-poh payr **fah**-ray ak-**kwee**-stee*

Is this the platform for Bologna?
E' questo il binario del treno per Bologna?
*e **kwe**-stoh eel bee-**nah**-ryoh dayl **tre**-noh payr boh-**loh**-nya*

Is there a left-luggage office?
C'è un deposito bagagli?
*che oon day-**po**-zee-toh ba-**ga**-lyee*

I want to leave these bags in the left-luggage
Voglio lasciare queste borse al deposito bagagli
***vo**-lyoh la-**shah**-ray **kwe**-stay **bohr**-say al day-**po**-zee-toh
  ba-**ga**-lyee1*

I shall pick them up this evening
Li torno a prendere questa sera
*lee **tohr**-noh a **prayn**-day-ray **kwe**-sta **say**-ra*

How much is it per bag?
Quanto si paga per borsa?
***kwan**-toh see **pa**-ga payr **bohr**-sa*

Are there any baggage trolleys?
Ci sono carrelli per il bagaglio?
*cee **soh**-noh kar-**rel**-lee payr eel ba-**ga**-lyoh*

Is this the Rome train?
E' questo il treno per Roma?
*e **kwe**-stoh eel **tre**-noh payr **roh**-ma*

Is there a buffet car?
C'é un vagone bar?
*che oon va-**goh**-nay bahr*

Is there a dining car?
C'é un vagone ristorante?
*che oon va-**goh**-nay ree-stoh-**ran**-tay*

By train

Is there a restaurant on the train?
C'è un vagone ristorante sul treno?
*che oon va-**goh**-nay ree-stoh-**ran**-tay sool **tre**-noh*

Is this a through train?
Devo cambiare treno?
***day**-voh kam-**byah**-ray **tre**-noh*

Do we stop at Cefalù?
Ci fermiamo a Cefalù?
*chee fayr-**myah**-moh a chay-fa-**loo***

What time do we get to Palermo?
A che ora arriviamo a Palermo?
*a kay **oh**-ra ar-ree-**vyah**-moh a pa-**layr**-moh*

Are we at Domodossola yet?
Non siamo ancora a Domodossola?
*nohn **syah**-moh an-**koh**-ra a Doh-moh-**dos**-soh-la*

Are we on time?
Siamo in orario?
***syah**-moh een oh-**rah**-ryoh*

Can you help me with my bags?
Mi può aiutare a portare le borse?
*mee pwo a-yoo-**tah**-ray a pohr-**tah**-ray lay **bohr**-say*

I have lost my ticket
Ho perso il biglietto
*oh **payr**-soh eel bee-**lyayt**-toh*

My wife has my ticket
Mia moglie ha il mio biglietto
*mee-a **moh**-lyay a eel **mee**-oh bee-**lyayt**-toh*

Is this seat taken?
E' occupato questo posto?
*e ohk-koo-**pah**-toh **kwe**-stoh **poh**-stoh*

This is my seat
Questo è il mio posto
***kwe**-stoh e eel **mee**-oh **poh**-stoh*

May I open the window?
Posso aprire il finestrino?
***pos**-soh a-**pree**-ray eel fee-nay-**stree**-noh*

This is a non-smoking compartment
Questo è uno scompartimento per non fumatori
***kwe**-stoh e **oo**-noh skohm-par-tee-**mayn**-toh payr nohn
foo-ma-**toh**-ree*

Where is the toilet?
Dov'è la toilette?
*doh-**ve** la toh-ee-**layt**-tay (twa-**let**)*

Why have we stopped?
Perché ci siamo fermati?
*payr-**kay** chee **syah**-moh fayr-**mah**-tee*

DRIVING

The main problem about driving in Italy is Italian driving. Many drivers are fast, impatient and generally inconsiderate of other road users, and some are seriously dangerous; the behaviour of motorway drivers can sometimes be very scary indeed. The southerners, particularly in Rome, Naples and Palermo, are the worst offenders – shooting through red traffic-lights, overtaking on the inside and incessantly using the horn. Other problems you may encounter on the roads are poorly signed exits, badly lit tunnels in mountainous areas and inconspicuous traffic-lights suspended over the centre of crossroads.

It's worth planning journeys to avoid the roads on holiday weekends, and to steer clear of the roads into major cities on Sunday evenings. (Sunday is otherwise a good day to travel, because of the lack of heavy lorries on the roads.)

On the plus side, there is a very extensive motorway network covering the country; tolls are charged, but they are not as high as those in France. The network of motorways (*autostrade*) in the north is particularly good, and some pass through magnificent scenery. Signposts indicating the way to a motorway are always in green. Tolls are charged according to the distance you travel and also vary with the size of your car. Normally you pick up a card on joining the motorway,

and pay on leaving it, but on some stretches you pay on joining the motorway.

Other roads are numbered and prefixed either with SS
(Strada Statale – first-class main road) or SP *(Strada Provin-
ciale* second-class through-road). The smaller roads, the
strada comunale, are sometimes very poorly surfaced.

Many main roads, including motorways, go through
mountainous country via an alternating series of bridges and
tunnels – and lighting in the tunnels is normally poor or non-
existent.

The rules

Driving on the right – this is not usually a problem as long
  as you don't follow your instinct to drive on the left-hand
  side when pulling out on to a deserted road.
Priority to the right – unless otherwise indicated, traffic
  coming from the right always has priority; this is mainly
  of relevance in the back streets of towns – on the open
  road, priority is normally indicated, as it is in Britain.
Use of horn – this is theoretically forbidden in most Italian
  cities (although it's a rule that is largely ignored by
  locals).
Headlights – dipped headlights must be used in tunnels.
Speed limits – in built-up areas 50km/hr (31mph); on
  country roads 110km/hr (68mph); on motorways 130km/
  hr (80mph). For camper vans the speed limit is 50km/hr in

built-up areas, 80km/hr on country roads and 100 km/hr
on motorways. Heavy on-the-spot fines are applied for
speeding.

Age limits – you have to be over 18 to drive a car, 21 if the
car can go at more than 180km/hr (112mph).

Safety belts – the use of belts is compulsory.

Drink-driving – fines for drunken driving are heavy, with
the additional possibility of six months' imprisonment, but
there is no official test or fixed blood-alcohol limit, and
there are many accidents caused by alcohol.

Traffic and weather conditions

Are there any hold-ups?
Ci sono ingorghi?
*chee **soh**-noh een-**gohr**-ghee*

Is the traffic heavy?
C'è molto traffico?
*che **mohl**-toh **traf**-fee-koh*

Is the traffic one-way?
E' una strada a senso unico?
*e **oo**-na **strah**-da a **sen**-soh **oo**-nee-koh*

Is there a different way to the stadium?
C'è un'altra strada per lo stadio?
*che oo-**nal**-tra **strah**-da payr loh **stah**-dyoh*

Traffic and weather conditions

Is there a toll on this motorway?
Si paga l'autostrada?
*see **pah**-ga la-oo-toh-**strah**-da*

What is causing this traffic jam?
Perché c'è quest'ingorgo?
*payr-**kay** che **kwe**-stin-**gohr**-goh*

What is the speed limit?
Qual è il limite di velocità?
*kwa-**le** eel **lee**-mee-tay dee vay-loh-chee-**ta***

When is the rush hour?
Quand'è l'ora di punta?
*kwan-**de** **loh**-ra dee **poon**-ta*

When will the road be clear?
Quando si libera la strada?
***kwan**-doh see **lee**-bay-ra la **strah**-da*

Is the pass open?
E' aperto il passo?
*e a-**per**-toh eel **pas**-soh*

Is the road to Sondrio snowed up?
La strada per Sondrio è chiusa per neve?
*la **strah**-da payr **sohn**-dree-oh e **kyoo**-za payr **nay**-vay*

Do I need snow chains?
Devo avere le catene?
***day**-voh a-**vay**-ray lay ka-**tay**-nay*

Parking

Parking is forbidden in a *zona verde* (green zone) and a *zona rimozione* (removal zone). Fines are high. You can park for a limited time in a *zona disco* or blue zone provided you display a disc. These can be purchased from petrol stations.

Italy is notorious for car thefts and break-ins. Never leave cars unlocked, windows open or any possessions visible inside. Where possible, leave your car in an attended garage.

Where is there a car park?
Dove c'é un parcheggio?
*doh-vay che oon par-**kayj**-joh*

Can I park here?
Posso parcheggiare qui?
*pos-soh par-kayj-**jah**-ray kwee*

Do I need a parking disc?
Devo mettere il disco orario?
*day-voh **mayt**-tay-ray eel **dee**-skoh oh-**rah**-ryoh*

Do I need coins for the meter?
Per il parchimetro occorre moneta?
*payr eel par-kee-**me**-tro oc-**cor**-ray moh-**nay**-ta*

Do I need parking lights?
Devo accendere i fari di posizione?
*day-voh a-chen-day-ray ee fa-ree dee poh-zee-**tsyoh**-ne*

How long can I stay here?
Quanto posso rimanere qui?
kwan-toh pos-soh ree-ma-nay-ray kwee

Is it safe to park here?
La macchina è sicura se parcheggio qui?
la mak-kee-na e see-koo-ra say par-kayj-joh kwee

What time does the car park close?
A che ora chiude il parcheggio?
a kay oh-ra kyoo-day eel par-kayj-joh

Where can I get a parking disc?
Dove posso comprare un disco orario?
doh-vay pos-soh kohm-prah-ray oon dee-skoh oh-rah-ryoh

Where do I pay?
Dove si paga?
doh-vay see pah-ga

At the service station

It's safer to specify how much petrol you want in euros than to ask for the tank to be filled. Many garages don't accept credit cards.

Do you take credit cards?
Accettate carte di credito?
a-chayt-tah-tay kar-tay dee kray-dee-toh

At the service station

Fill the tank please
Faccia il pieno, per favore
*fa-cha eel **pye**-noh, payr fa-**voh**-ray*

25 litres of— diesel
Venticinque litri di — gasolio
*vayn-tee-**cheen**-kway **lee**-tree dee — ga-**zo**-lyoh*

— unleaded petrol
— benzina senza piombo
*—bayn-**dzee**-na **sen**-tsa
pyohm-boh*

— 3 star
— 3 stelle
*— tray **stay**-lay*

— 4 star
— 4 stelle
*— **kwat**-troh **stay**-lay*

Check the tyre pressure please
Controlli la pressione delle gomme per piacere
*kohn-**trohl**-lee la prays-**syo**-nay **day**-lay **gohm**-may payr
pya-**chay**-ray*

The pressure should be 2.3 at the front and 2.5 at the rear
La pressione dovrebbe essere due virgola tre (2,3) davanti e
due virgola cinque (2,5) di dietro
*la prays-**syoh**-nay doh-**vrayb**-bay es-say-ray **doo**-ay **veer**-goh-la
tray da-**van**-tee ay **doo**-ay **veer**-goh-la **cheen**-kway dee
dye-troh*

Check — the oil
Controlli — l'olio
*kohn-**trohl**-lee — **lo**-lyoh*

— the water
— l'acqua
— ***lak**-kwa*

Can you clean the windscreen?
Può pulire il parabrezza?
*pwo poo-**lee**-ray eel pa-ra-**braydz**-za*

I need some distilled water
Ho bisogno di acqua distillata
*oh bee-**zoh**-nyoh de **ak**-kwa dee-steel-**lah**-ta*

Breakdowns and repairs

A red warning triangle must be placed at least 50 yards behind a broken-down car. These are compulsory equipment, and can be bought in Britain or hired temporarily at the frontier.

In case of breakdown on an ordinary road, telephone 116, which is the emergency 24-hour number for English-speaking assistance. Tell the operator where you are, the registration number and type of car: On motorways there are telephones every 2km, connected to an emergency service.

Any tourist travelling in Italy can use the Automobile Club

Breakdowns and repairs

d'Italia (ACI) breakdown service for a fee. If you join the ACI you will qualify for a discount. The ACI can assist you in finding a garage to repair your car. The address of the ACI is Via Marsala 8, 00185 Rome.

Is there a telephone nearby?
C'è un telefono qui vicino?
*che oon tay-**lay**-foh-noh kwee vee-**chee**-noh*

Can you send a recovery truck?
Potete mandare un carro-attrezzi?
*poh-**tay**-tay man-**dah**-ray oon **kar**-roh at-**trets**-zee*

Can you take me to the nearest garage?
Mi può portare al garage più vicino?
*mee pwo pohr-**tah**-ray al ga-**raj** pyoo vee-**chee**-noh*

Can you give me a push?
Mi può dare una spinta?
*mee pwo **dah**-ray oo-na **speen**-ta*

Can you give me a can of petrol?
Mi può dare una latta di benzina?
*mee pwo **dah**-ray oo-na **lat**-ta dee bayn-**dzee**-na*

Can you give me a tow?
Può trainarmi?
*pwo tra-ee-**nahr**-mee*

Is there a mechanic here?
C'è un meccanico qui?
*che oon mayk-**kah**-nee-koh kwee*

Breakdowns and repairs

Can you repair a flat tyre?
Può riparare una gomma bucata?
*pwo ree-pa-**rah**-ray **oo**-na **gohm**-ma boo-**kah**-ta*

Can you repair it for the time being?
Può fare una riparazione provvisoria?
*pwo **fah**-ray **oo**-na ree-pa-ra-**tsyoh**-nay prohv-vee-**zoh**-rya*

Can you replace the windscreen wiper blades?
Può sostituire le spazzole del tergicristallo?
*pwo soh-stee-too-**ee**-ray lay spats-**tsoh**-lay **dayl**
tayr-jee-kree-**stal**-loh*

I have locked the ignition key inside the car
Ho chiuso la chiave di avviamento dentro la macchina
*oh **kyoo**-zoh la **kyah**-vay dee av-vya-**mayn**-toh **dayn**-troh la
mak-kee-na*

Do you have an emergency fan belt?
Ha una cinghia di emergenza per la ventola?
*a **oo**-na **cheen**-gya dee ay-mayr-**jen**-tsa payr la **vayn**-toh-la*

I need a new fan belt
Mi occorre una cinghia nuova per la ventola
*mee oc-**cor**-ray **oo**-na **cheen**-gya **nwo**-va payr la **vayn**-toh-la*

Do you have jump leads?
Ha i cavi per collegare due batterie?
*a ee **kah**-vee payr cohl-lay-**gah**-ray **doo**-ay bat-tay-**ree**-ay*

Breakdowns and repairs

There is something wrong
C'è qualcosa che non va
che kwal-ko-za kay nohn va

Can you find out what the trouble is?
Può dirmi qual è il problema?
pwo deer-mee kwa-le eel proh-ble-ma

There is something wrong with the car
La macchina ha qualche cosa che non va
la mak-kee-na a kwal-kay ko-za kay nohn va

Will it take long to repair it?
Quanto ci vorrà per ripararla?
kwan-toh chee vohr-ra payr ree-pa-rar-la

Do you have the spare parts?
Ha i pezzi di ricambio?
a ee pets-see dee ree-kam-byoh

I have a flat tyre
Ho una gomma a terra
oh oo-na gohm-ma a ter-ra

I have blown a fuse
Si è bruciato un fusibile
see e broo-chah-toh oon foo-zee-bee-lay

I have locked myself out of the car
Mi sono chiuso fuori della macchina
mee soh-noh kyoo-zoh fwoh-ree day-la mak-kee-na

I have run out of petrol
Ho finito la benzina
oh fee-nee-toh la bayn-dzee-na

I think there is a bad connection
Penso che ci sia un contatto difettoso
payn-soh kay chee see-a oon kohn-tat-toh dee-fayt-toh-zoh

My car has been towed away
Mi hanno trainato via la macchina
mee an-noh tra-ee-nah-toh vee-a la mak-kee-na

My car has broken down
Ho la macchina in panne
oh la mak-kee-na een pan

My car will not start
La macchina non parte
la mak-kee-na nohn par-tay

My windscreen has cracked
Mi si è rotto il parabrezza
mee see e roht-toh eel pa-ra-braydz-za

The air-conditioning does not work
L'aria condizionata non funziona
la-rya kohn-dee-tsyoh-nah-ta nohn foon-tsyoh-na

The battery is flat
La batteria è morta
la bat-tay-ree-a e mor-ta

Accidents and the police

The engine has broken down
Il motore si è fermato
*eel moh-**toh**-ray see e fayr-**mah**-toh*

The engine is overheating
Il motore surriscalda
*eel moh-**toh**-ray soor-ree-**skal**-da*

The exhaust pipe has fallen off
E' caduto il tubo dello scappamento
*e ka-**doo**-toh eel **too**-boh **dayl**-loh skap-pa-**mayn**-toh*

There is a leak in the radiator
C'è una perdita nel radiatore
*che **oo**-na **payr**-dee-ta nayl ra-dya-**toh**-ray*

Accidents and the police

There has been an accident
C'è stato un incidente
*che **stah**-toh oon een-chee-**den**-tay*

We must call — an ambulance
Dobbiamo chiamare — un'ambulanza
*dohb-**byah**-moh kya-**mah**-ray — oo-nam-boo-**lan**-tsa*

— the police
— la polizia
*— la poh-lee-**tsee**-a*

What is your name and address?
Mi dà il suo nome e indirizzo?
*mee da eel **soo**-oh **noh**-may ay een-dee-**reets**-soh*

You must not move
Non vi dovete muovere
*nohn vee doh-**vay**-tay **mwo**-vay-ray*

He did not stop
Non si è fermato
*nohn see e fayr-**mah**-toh*

He is a witness
Lui è testimone
*loo-ee e tay-stee-**moh**-nay*

He overtook on a bend
Ha superato in curva
*a soo-pay-**rah**-toh een **koor**-va*

He ran into the back of my car
Mi è venuto addosso da dietro
*mee e vay-**noo**-toh ad-**dos**-soh da **dye**-troh*

He stopped suddenly
Si è fermato all'improvviso
*see e fayr-**mah**-toh al-leem-prohv-**vee**-soh*

He was moving too fast
Andava troppo veloce
*an-**dah**-va **trop**-poh vay-**loh**-chay*

Accidents and the police

I was overtaking
Stavo superando
stah-voh soo-pay-ran-doh

I was parking
Stavo parcheggiando
stah-voh par-kayj-jan-doh

That car was too close
Quella macchina era troppo vicina
kwayl-la mak-kee-na ay-ra trop-poh vee-chee-na

The brakes failed
I freni non hanno funzionato
ee fray-nee nohn an-noh foon-tsyoh-nah-toh

The car number was . . .
La targa della macchina era . . .
la tar-ga dayl-la mak-kee-na ay-ra . . .

The car skidded
La macchina ha slittato
la mak-kee-na a sleet-tah-toh

The car swerved
La macchina ha sbandato
la mak-kee-na a sban-dah-toh

The car turned right without signalling
La macchina ha girato a destra senza mettere la freccia
*la mak-kee-na a jee-rah-toh a de-stra sen-tsa mayt-tay-ray
la fray-cha*

Accidents and the police

The road was icy
La strada era ghiacciata
la strah-da ay-ra gya-chah-ta

The tyre burst
E' scoppiata la gomma
e skohp-pyah-ta la gohm-ma

I could not stop in time
Non sono riuscito a fermarmi in tempo
nohn soh-noh ree-oo-shee-toh a fayr-mahr-mee een tem-poh

I did not see the bicycle
Non ho visto la bicicletta
nohn oh vee-stoh la bee-chee-clayt-ta

I did not see the sign
Non ho visto l'indicazione
nohn oh vee-stoh lin-dee-cats-zee-oh-nay

I did not know about the speed limit
Non sapevo ci fosse un limite di velocità
*nohn sa-pay-voh chee fohs-say oon lee-mee-tay dee
  vay-loh-chee-ta*

Here are my insurance documents
Ecco i documenti dell'assicurazione
ek-koh ee doh-koo-mayn-tee dayl-las-see-koo-ra-tsyoh-nay

Here is my driving licence
Ecco la patente
ek-koh la pa-ten-tay

Accidents and the police

Do you want my credit card?
Vuole la mia carta di credito?
*vwo-lay la **mee**-a **kar**-ta dee **kray**-dee-toh*

Do you want my passport?
Vuole il mio passaporto?
*vwo-lay eel **mee**-oh pas-sa-**por**-toh*

How much is the fine?
Quanto è la multa?
***kwan**-toh e la **mool**-ta*

I have not got enough money. Can I pay at the police station?
Non ho abbastanza soldi. Posso pagare alla centrale di polizia?
*nohn oh ab-ba-**stan**-tsa **sol**-dee. **pos**-soh pa-**gah**-ray al-la chayn-**trah**-lay dee poh-lee-**tsee**-a*

I am very sorry. I am a visitor
Mi dispiace. Sono un turista
*mee dee-**spyah**-chay. **soh**-noh oon too-**ree**-sta*

I did not understand the sign
Non ho capito il segnale
*nohn oh ka-**pee**-toh eel say-**nyah**-lay*

I have not had anything to drink
Non ho bevuto niente
*nohn oh bay-**voo**-toh **nyen**-tay*

I was only driving at 50 km/h
Guidavo solo a cinquanta all'ora
*gwee-**dah**-voh **soh**-loh a cheen-**kwan**-ta al-**loh**-ra*

Road signs and notices

deviazione
*day-vee-a-**tsyoh**-nay*
diversion

mantenere la destra
*man-tay-**nay**-ray la **de**-stra*
keep to the right

strada privata
***strah**-da pree-**vah**-ta*
private road

vietato entrare
*vyay-**tah**-toh ayn-**trah**-ray*
no entry

vietato l'accesso
*vyay-**tah**-toh la-**ches**-soh*
no thoroughfare

corsia per biciclette
*kohr-see-a payr bee-chee-**klayt**-tay*
cycle path

Car parts

parcheggio riservato ai residenti
par-kayj-joh ree-zayr-vah-toh a-ee ray-zee-den-tee
parking for residents only

Car parts

accelerator
acceleratore
a-chay-lay-ra-toh-ray

aerial
antenna
an-tayn-na

air filter
filtro dell'aria
feel-troh dayl-lah-rya

alternator
alternatore
al-tayr-na-toh-ray

antifreeze
antigelo
an-tee-jay-loh

automatic gearbox
cambio automatico
kam-byoh a-oo-toh-ma-tee-koh

axle
assale
as-sah-lay

battery
batteria
bat-tay-ree-a

bonnet
cofano
ko-fa-noh

boot
portabagagli
pohr-ta-ba-ga-lyee

brake fluid
liquido dei freni
lee-kwee-doh day-ee fray-nee

brakes
freni
fray-nee

bulb
lampadina
lam-pa-dee-na

bumper
paraurti
pa-ra-oor-tee

car-phone
telefono in macchina
tay-lay-foh-noh een
  mak-kee-na

carburettor
carburatore
kar-boo-ra-toh-ray

child seat
sedile per bambini
say-dee-lay payr bam-bee-nee

choke
aria
ah-rya

clutch
frizione
free-tsyoh-nay

cooling system
raffreddamento
raf-frayd-da-mayn-toh

cylinder
cilindro
chee-leen-droh

disc brake
freno a disco
fray-noh a dee-skoh

distributor
spinterogeno
speen-tay-ro-jay-noh

door
portiera / sportello
pohr-tye-ra / spohr-tel-loh

dynamo
dinamo
dee-na-moh

electrical system
impianto elettrico
eem-pyan-toh ay-let-tree-koh

engine
motore
moh-toh-ray

exhaust system
sistema di scappamento
sees-te-ma dee
  skap-pa-mayn-toh

Car parts

fan belt
cinghia della ventola
cheen-gya dayl-la vayn-toh-la

foot pump
pompa meccanica
pohm-pa mayk-ka-nee-ka

fuel gauge
indicatore della benzina
*een-dee-ka-toh-ray dayl-la
  bayn-dzee-na*

fuse
fusibile
foo-zee-bee-lay

fuel pump
pompa della benzina
pohm-pa dayl-la bayn-dzee-na

gear box
scatola del cambio
skah-toh-la dayl kam-byoh

gear lever
leva del cambio
le-va dayl kam-byoh

generator
dinamo
dee-na-moh

hammer
martello
mar-tel-loh

hand brake
freno a mano
fray-noh a mah-noh

hazard lights
luci di pericolo
loo-chee dee pay-ree-koh-loh

headlights
fari
fah-ree

heating system
riscaldamento
ree-skal-da-mayn-toh

hood
capote
ka-pot

horn
clacson
klak-sohn

hose
manica
mah-nee-ka

110

ignition
avviamento
*av-vya-**mayn**-toh*

ignition key
chiave di avviamento
*kyah-vay dee av-vya-**mayn**-toh*

indicator
freccia
fray-cha

jack
crick
kreek

lights
luci
loo-chee

lock
serratura
*sayr-ra-**too**-ra*

oil filter
filtro dell'olio
*feel-troh dayl-**lo**-lyoh*

oil
olio
o-lyoh

oil pressure
pressione dell'olio
*prays-**syoh**-nay dayl-**lo**-lyoh*

petrol
benzina
*bayn-**dzee**-na*

points
puntine
*poon-**tee**-nay*

pump
pompa
pohm-pa

radiator
radiatore
*ra-dya-**toh**-ray*

rear view mirror
specchio retrovisore
*spek-kyoh ray-troh-vee-**zoh**-ray*

reflectors
catarifrangenti
*ka-ta-ree-fran-**jayn**-te*

roof-rack
portabagagli sul tetto
*pohr-ta-ba-**ga**-lyee sool*
 tayt-toh

Car parts

screwdriver
cacciavite
ca-cha-vee-tay

seat belt
cinghia di sicurezza
*cheen-gya dee
  see-koo-rayts-sah*

seat
sedile
say-dee-lay

shock absorber
ammortizzatore
am-mohr-tits-sa-toh-ray

silencer
silenziatore
see-lent-see-a-toh-ray

spanner
chiave inglese
kyah-vay een-glay-say

spare part
pezzo di ricambio
pets-soh dee ree-kam-byoh

spark plug
candela
kan-day-la

speedometer
tachimetro
ta-kee-may-troh

starter motor
motorino d'avviamento
*moh-toh-ree-noh
  dav-vya-mayn-toh*

steering
sterzo
ster-tsoh

steering wheel
volante
voh-lan-tay

stoplight
luce d'arresto / stop
loo-chay dar-re-stoh / stop

sun roof
tetto apribile
tayt-toh a-pree-bee-lay

suspension
sospensione
soh-spayn-syoh-nay

tools
attrezzi
at-trayts-see

towbar
asta di rimorchio
as-ta dee ree-mohr-kyoh

transmission
trasmissione
tras-mees-syoh-nay

trunk
portabagagli
pohr-ta-ba-ga-lyee

tyre
gomma
gohm-ma

warning light
luce di emergenza
loo-chay dee e-mer-jen-za

water
acqua
ak-kwa

wheel
ruota
rwo-ta

windscreen
parabrezza
pa-ra-braydz-za

windshield
parabrezza
pa-ra-braydz-za

wipers
tergicristallo
tayr-jee-kree-stal-loh

EATING OUT

Restaurants

Eating out is a favourite Italian pastime. A substantial proportion of the family budget is spent on food, and it's quite normal for the entire family, granny and toddlers included, to go out for lunch on Sundays and public holidays. There are eating places to suit all tastes and pockets, from humble cafés to very elegant restaurants.

Traditionally, there are three main categories of restaurant: a *ristorante* is a formal restaurant, grander than a *trattoria* (usually a family-run, fairly simple restaurant), which in turn is smarter than an *osteria*. But the distinctions are becoming more and more blurred – you may, for example, find a rustic-looking *osteria* to be chic and pricey.

For simple straightforward food, the best place is a *pizzeria* (which usually serves more than just pizzas) or a snack bar. A *tavola calda* provides both hot and cold food – either to eat on the premises or to take away – displayed behind glass and usually priced by weight. A *rosticceria*, originally a shop specializing in grilled meats, chicken and fish, may have tables where you can sit down and eat. Bars often serve snacks.

Choosing a restaurant

Restaurant guidebooks are not as influential in Italy as in France or even Britain, and they are not as useful when choosing where to eat. If you turn to the guides for help, you may overlook excellent places right under your nose.

The first rule is to avoid the main sights and piazzas of tourist towns and the sea fronts of popular resorts and to seek out the family-run *trattorie* in back streets, preferably those full of local-looking Italians. Look for menus (which will be in the window or inside the door) that are entirely in Italian. Some of the best-value places don't have a menu at all; ask what's good today, and see what turns up. The setting may be uninspiring but decor in Italy is no guide to culinary standards.

If you want to be sure of not missing the culinary high spots, you will need a restaurant guide. The *Michelin Red Guide* is not as reliable for Italy as it is for France but is a useful point of reference, recommending thousands of different restaurants throughout the country. The two-line entries are crammed with hieroglyphics, which take some getting used to but don't require you to understand any Italian.

Beware the advice of hoteliers (or hotel staff) on where to eat; their cousin Luigi's place may be the best around but may not.

Food

Although the French don't like to admit it, their *haute cuisine* was originally imported from Italy – or at least was greatly influenced by the Italians. The crucial event was the arrival in the 16th century of the Italian-born Catherine of Medici, who brought her team of Florentine chefs, schooled in the subtleties of Renaissance cooking. Today the accent is not so much on elaborate and formal dishes but on simplicity and fresh local produce. A memorable meal is more likely to be a subtle regional dish based on local specialities (and probably including pasta) than a refined gastronomic treat. And you are more likely to find it in a family-run *trattoria* than in a sophisticated restaurant.

The traditional regional divisions of Italy have ensured that regional specialities still play a major role in Italian cooking. The variation of climate and terrain produces a wide range of ingredients, many of which are used in pasta or rice dishes. Food tends to be more refined the farther north you go. Northern Italy is known for its creamy sauces, butter and garlic-based dishes, meat and risottos, the south for pizzas, tomato sauces and deep-fried fish.

Regional specialities

Piedmont
One of the regions of the north generally considered to be the best for food – heavily influenced by the neighbouring French. Specialities include *fonduta* (hot dip with cheese, eggs and sometimes white truffles), *bolliti misti con salsa verde* (boiled meats with green herb sauce), *cardi in bagna cauda* – edible thistles with a sauce of anchovies, cream and garlic.

Trentino-Alto Adige
The accent here is on Austrian-style food such as *speck* (smoked raw ham), *selchcaree mit kraut* (smoked pork with sauerkraut), dumplings, sausages and heavy potato-based pies.

Trieste area
The region offers a variety of cooking, with Austrian and Slav as well as Italian dishes. Trieste and Grado are good for seafood. San Daniele del Friuli is famous for its raw and smoked hams. Popular soups are *minestra di fagioli,* with beans, and a sauerkraut soup known as *la jota.*

Lombardy
In Lombardy, you will find a great deal of variation in the cuisine, particularly between the rural and urban areas.

Regional specialities

Around the lakes, fish is often a better bet than meat. Types you are likely to come across are perch, tench, eel and various kinds of trout – often marinated with herbs and fried.

Emilia-Romagna

This is one of the more gastronomic regions of Italy – particularly for hams, sausages and salamis. Bologna in particular is well known for its pasta and meat dishes. Parma is noted for hams and cheese, also for pastas. Modena's main speciality is *zampone* – stuffed pigs' trotters. Along the coast you can find plenty of places serving mixed fried fish and *brodetto* – a fish soup.

Rome and Lazio

Rome has an endless variety of pasta dishes, and often the pasta is home-made. Other specialities include *carciofi alla Giudea* (artichokes fried in olive oil) and *piselli al prosciutto* (peas cooked with bacon and ham).

Liguria (Italian Riviera)

There is a wide choice of fish and seafood along the coast. The main soup speciality is *burrida*, similar to the French *bouillabaisse*. *Focaccia* is a snack of bread-like dough with onions, tomatoes and other savoury flavourings, served hot. *Torta pasqualina* is a vegetable pie with eggs, cheese and mushrooms.

Venice and the Veneto

In Venice, fish is usually a safer bet than meat, although it's

Regional specialities

quite often frozen. Specialities include *seppie* (cuttlefish).
San Pietro (John Dory) and *anguilla* (eel). Specialities of the
Veneto include game and poultry, pigeon soup and *baccalà*
(salt cod). You'll often see polenta – boiled maize, served in
(often rather rubbery) slices.

Tuscany and Umbria

Among the specialities of the inland regions are poultry,
game, small birds, mountain hams and soups. Fish dishes are
popular around Livorno. Umbria is best known for its truffles, served with spaghetti or on *crostini*, and for *porchetta*
(roast suckling pig). Other specialities include *pappardelle
con la lepre* (pasta with hare sauce), *ribollita* (Florentine
soup of white beans, olive oil and other ingredients),
bruschetta or *fettunta* (bread fried in olive oil with garlic and
sometimes chopped tomatoes), *bongo-bongo* (profiteroles)
and *panforte* (spicy cake from Siena).

Naples and Campania

The Naples area is the home of the pizza. There are endless
varieties, including the ubiquitous *pizza alla napoletana* –
with mozzarella cheese, tomatoes, olives and anchovy fil-
lets. The cheese used on pizza, *mozzarella* (which is made
from buffalo milk), is commonly used in other dishes too –
such as *mozzarella in carrozza* (cheese sandwich dipped in
egg and fried).

Excellent fish and seafood is served all along the coast, either with pasta, on pizzas, in soups or as a main fish dish.

Regional specialities

Uncooked shellfish is not recommended because of heavy pollution in the Bay of Naples.

The deep south

Olive oil and a variety of fresh vegetables and fruit are the mainstays of Apulian cookery. *Ostriche* (oysters), *cozze* (mussels) and other seafood are its specialities, also roast lamb and *calzone,* a folded pasta. In Basilicata and Calábria, aubergines are cooked in a variety of ways, e.g. *melanzane ripiene* (stuffed and baked) or *melanzane sott'olio* (marinated with oil, garlic and peppers). Calabria has roast kid and fresh trout from the mountain streams.

Sicily

The main specialities are fish and vegetables. Something cooked alla *Siciliana* usually means with tomatoes, red peppers, onions, capers and herbs; *caponata* is a vegetable dish similar to the French *ratatouille*. The main pasta speciality is *con sarde* – with sardine sauce. There are many pastry and dessert specialities of which the most famous is *cassata siciliana*.

Sardinia

There is plenty of fish around the coasts but the local specialities are from the inland mountain areas: *porchetta* (suckling pig), *cinghiale* (wild boar), *agnello* (lamb) and *carta da musica* (very thin bread eaten with oil and salt).

Meals and menus

For most Italians, lunch is the main meal of the day, and shops and offices tend to close down for a couple of hours. Most restaurants are open for lunch from 12.30pm to 3.00pm. Southerners tend to eat dinner later than northerners – in Rome its normal to dine at 9.00pm, in Milan 7.30pm or 8.00pm is more common. Most restaurants close one day a week, often Monday.

A normal menu will offer the possibility of four or five courses: *antipasto* (the equivalent of hors d'oeuvres), *pasta, minestre* (soups), *secondi platti* (main courses) and *dolci* (dessert). (Cheese does not normally constitute a course, but will be available if you ask.)

It is not unusual to take only a couple of courses in a restaurant. Although most restaurants prefer you to order a main course, there is no reason why you should not opt for an *antipasto* followed by a pasta or even just a pasta followed by a salad. One-course customers are not so popular.

It is common practice to take orders for only the first two courses to start with, and to take main-course orders later:

All-in fixed-price meals are neither as common nor as uniformly attractive as they are in France, for example. Tourist menus, which offer a 2- or 3-course meal at an all-inclusive fixed price (sometimes with wine, beer or soft drink thrown in) are usually a cheap way of combating hunger rather than

Meals and menus

a pleasurable experience – a typical *menu turistico* might be spaghetti, followed by roast chicken and ice-cream or fruit. But fixed-price menus in more expensive restaurants can be excellent and good value.

The first courses of restaurant meals are almost always the most interesting part. An *antipasto* might be a plate of cold meats such as salami, ham and mortadella, for example. *Antipasto misto*, the Italian version of hors d'oeuvre, is usually a colourful display including marinated vegetables, various seafood dishes, cold meats, artichokes and more.

Fresh fish soups can be delicious and they're often filling enough to have as a main course. But, sadly, fresh fish is becoming increasingly scarce along the coasts, and when you do see it prices are always high.

Pasta is something that even the most touristy restaurant will often serve well – perhaps because it is often at its best with the simplest, least expensive sauces.

The main course is often an unappetising lump of meat with no garnish. Vegetables are always served separately, and work out very expensive – and the choice can be disappointing, given the huge variety you see in the markets. Don't be surprised if the vegetables are served cold. Side salads often include *radicchio* (red chicory), lettuce, carrot or tomato.

Desserts are often limited. Fruit often makes the most refreshing choice after a copious Italian meal: the range in summer includes peaches, apricots, figs and watermelon.

Ice-cream is often home-made and hard to resist – as is the chilled ice-cream cake called *semifreddo*. In more elaborate places you may find a choice of more sophisticated fare, with gateaux and pastries.

Prices

When looking at the prices on a menu, bear in mind that cover and service charges may well increase your bill by 15 to 20 per cent. The size of the cover charge is a good guide to the level of prices as a whole. The main exception is the *menu turistico* which should have no extras to pay.

For the pleasure of eating *al fresco* you will normally pay substantially more than in a restaurant where there's no outdoor terrace.

Reservations

Should we reserve a table?
Dobbiamo prenotare un tavolo?
dohb-byah-moh pray-noh-tah-ray oon tah-voh-loh

Can I book a table for four at 8 o'clock?
Posso prenotare un tavolo per quattro per le otto?
pos-soh pray-noh-tah-ray oon ta-voh-loh payr kwat-troh payr lay ot-toh

Useful questions

We would like a table — by the window
Vorremmo un tavolo — vicino alla finestra
*vohr-**rem**-moh oon **tah**-voh-loh — vee-**chee**-noh **al**-la*
*fee-**ne**-stra*

— on the terrace
— sulla terrazza
— ***sool**-la tayr-**rats**-sa*

Where can we sit down?
Dove ci possiamo sedere?
***doh**-vay chee pohs-**syah**-moh say-**day**-ray*

Can we have a table for four?
Possiamo avere un tavolo per quattro?
*pos-**syah**-moh a-**vay**-ray oon **tah**-voh-loh payr **kwat**-troh*

I am a vegetarian
Sono vegetariano
***soh**-noh vay-jay-ta-**ryah**-noh*

Useful questions

Do you have a set menu?
Avete un menù fisso?
*a-**vay**-tay oon may-**noo fees**-soh*

Are vegetables included?
Le verdure sono comprese?
*lay vayr-**doo**-ray **soh**-noh kohm-**pray**-say*

Useful questions

Do you have a local speciality?
Avete una specialità locale?
a-vay-tay *oo*-na spay-cha-lee-*ta* loh-*kah*-lay

How do I eat this?
Come si mangia questo?
koh-may see *man*-ja *kwe*-stoh

Is the local wine good?
E' buono il vino di qui?
e *bwo*-noh eel *vee*-noh dee kwee

Is this cheese very strong?
Questo formaggio è molto forte?
kwe-stoh fohr-*maj*-joh e *mohl*-toh *for*-tay

Do you have yoghurt?
Avete yogurt?
a-vay-tay *yo*-goort

Is this good?
E' buono questo?
e *bwo*-noh *kwe*-stoh

What do you recommend?
Che cosa ci consiglia?
kay *ko*-za chee kohn-*see*-lya

What is the dish of the day?
Qual'è il piatto del giorno?
kwa-*le* eel *pyat*-toh dayl *johr*-noh

Useful questions

What is the soup of the day?
Qual'è la minestra del giorno?
kwa-le la mee-ne-stra dayl johr-noh

What is this called?
Come si chiama questo?
koh-may see kyah-ma kwe-stoh

What is this dish like?
Com'è questo piatto?
koh-me kwe-stoh pyat-toh

Which local wine do you recommend?
Quale vino locale consigliate?
kwa-le vee-noh loh-kah-lay kohn-see-lyah-tay

Can I have an ashtray?
Mi dà un portacenere?
mee da oon pohr-ta-chay-nay-ray

Can we have some bread?
Possiamo avere dell'altro pane?
pohs-syah-moh a-vay-ray dayl-lal-troh pah-nay

Could we have some butter?
Possiamo avere del burro?
pohs-syah-moh a-vay-ray dayl boor-roh

Could we have some more bread please?
Possiamo avere dell'altro pane, per favore?
*pohs-syah-moh a-vay-ray dayl-lal-troh pah-nay, payr
  fa-voh-ray*

Ordering your meal

The menu, please
Il menù, per piacere
*eel may-**noo**, payr pya-**chay**-ray*

Can we start with soup?
Possiamo incominciare con una minestra?
*pohs-**syah**-moh een-koh-meen-**chah**-ray kohn **oo**-na mee-**ne**-stra*

I will take the set menu
Prendo il menù fisso
***prayn**-doh eel may-**noo fees**-soh*

I like my steak — very rare
Vorrei una bistecca — al sangue
*vor-**ray**-ee una bee-**stayk**-ka la — al **san**-gway*

— medium rare
— cotta giusta
— ***kot**-ta **joo**-sta*

— rare
— poco cotta
— ***poh**-koh **kot**-ta*

— well done
— ben cotta
— *bayn **kot**-ta*

Ordering drinks

I will have salad
Prendo un'insalata
prayn-doh oo-neen-sa-lah-ta

That is for me
Quello è per me
kwayl-loh e payr may

I will take that
Prendo questo
prayn-doh kwe-stoh

Can I see the menu again, please?
Posso vedere un'altra volta il menù, per favore?
*pos-soh vay-day-ray oo-nal-tra vol-ta eel may-noo, payr
fa-voh-ray*

Ordering drinks

The wine list, please
La lista dei vini, per piacere?
la lee-sta day-ee vee-nee, payr pya-chay-ray

A bottle of house red wine, please
Una bottiglia di vino rosso della casa, per piacere
*oo-na boht-tee-lya dee vee-noh rohs-soh dayl-la kah-za,
payr pya-chay-ray*

A glass of dry white wine, please
Un bicchiere di vino bianco secco, per piacere
oon beek-kye-ray dee vee-noh byan-koh sayk-koh, payr
pya-chay-ray

We will take the Chianti
Prendiamo il Chianti
prayn-dyah-moh eel kyan-tee

Another bottle of red wine, please
Un'altra bottiglia di vino rosso, per piacere
oo-nal-tra boht-tee-lya dee vee-noh rohs-soh, payr
pya-chay-ray

Another glass, please
Un altro bicchiere, per favore
oon al-troh beek-kye-ray, payr fa-voh-ray

Black coffee, please
Un caffè, per favore
oon kaf-fe, payr fa-voh-ra

Can we have some mineral water?
Possiamo avere dell'acqua minerale?
pohs-syah-moh a-vay-ray dayl-lak-kwa mee-nay-rah-lay

Coffee with milk, please
Un caffè col latte / macchiato, per favore
oon kaf-fe cohl lat-tay / ma-chee-a-toh, payr fa-voh-ray

Paying the bill

Some plain water, please
Dell'acqua di rubinetto, per piacere
dayl-lak-kwa dee roo-bee-nayt-toh, payr pya-chay-ray

Two beers, please
Due birre, per favore
doo-ay beer-ray, payr fa-voh-ray

Paying the bill

Can we have the bill, please?
Ci porta il conto per favore?
chee pohr-ta eel kohn-toh payr fa-voh-ray

I would like to pay with my credit card
Vorrei pagare con la carta di credito
vor-re-ee pa-gah-ray kohn la kar-ta dee kray-dee-toh

Is service included?
Il servizio è compreso?
eel sayr-vee-tsyoh e kohm-pray-zoh

Is tax included?
La tassa è compresa?
la tas-sa e kohm-pray-za

Is there any extra charge?
Ci sono sovrapprezzi?
chee soh-noh soh-vrap-prets-see

Complaints and compliments

This is not correct
Questo non è giusto
kwe-stoh nohn e joo-stoh

This is not my bill
Questo non è il mio conto
kwe-stoh nohn e eel mee-oh kohn-toh

I do not have enough money
Non ho abbastanza soldi
nohn oh ab-ba-stan-tsa sol-dee

Complaints and compliments

This is cold
Questo è freddo
kwe-stoh e frayd-doh

This is not what I ordered
Non è quello che ho ordinato
nohn e kwayl-loh kay oh ohr-dee-nah-toh

Waiter! We have been waiting for a long time.
Cameriere, è un pezzo che aspettiamo.
kam-ay-ryay-ray, e oon pet-soh kay as-payt-tyah-moh

Can I have the recipe?
Posso avere la ricetta?
pos-soh a-vay-ray la ree-chet-ta

Menu reader

The meal was excellent
Abbiamo mangiato benissimo
*ab-**byah**-moh man-**jah**-toh bay-**nees**-see-moh*

This is excellent
Questo è ottimo
kwe-stoh e ot-tee-moh

Menu reader

aceto
*a-**chay**-toh*
vinegar

aglio
a-lyoh
garlic

albicocche
*al-bee-**kok**-kay*
apricots

alla griglia
*al-la **gree**-lyah*
grilled/barbecued

ananas
a-na-nas
pineapple

anatra
ah-na-tra
duck

anguria
*an-**goo**-rya*
watermelon

aragosta
*a-ra-**goh**-sta*
lobster

arance
*a-**ran**-chay*
oranges

arrosto di maiale
*ar-**ro**-stoh dee ma-**yah**-lay*
pork roast

asparagi
as-pah-ra-jee
asparagus

avocado
a-voh-kah-doh
avocado

baccalà
bak-ka-la
salt cod

banane
ba-nah-nay
bananas

barbabietola
bar-ba-bye-toh-la
beetroot

barbabietole
bar-ba-bye-toh-lay
beetroot

basilico
ba-zee-lee-koh
basil

bistecca
bee-stayk-ka
beefsteak

bistecca di filetto
bee-stayk-ka dee fee-layt-toh
steak fillet

bomboloni
bohm-boh-loh-nee
doughnuts

brodo di manzo
bro-doh dee man-dzoh
beef broth

brodo di pollo
bro-doh dee pohl-lo
chicken broth

burro
boor-roh
butter

calamari
ka-la-mah-ree
squid

carciofi
kar-cho-fee
artichokes

carne alla griglia
kar-nay al-la gree-lya
grilled meats

Menu reader

carne
kahr-nay
meat

carote
ka-ro-tay
carrots

cavolfiore
ka-vohl-fyoh-ray
cauliflower

cavolini di Bruxelles
kah-voh-lee-nee dee broo-sayl-lay
Brussels sprouts

cavolo
kah-voh-loh
cabbage

cefalo
che-fa-loh
mullet

cerfoglio
chayr-fo-lyoh
chervil

cetriolo
chay-tree-o-loh
cucumber

ciliege
chee-lye-jay
cherries

cioccolata
chohk-koh-lah-ta
chocolate

cipolla
chee-pohl-la
onion

composta di mele
kohm-poh-sta dee may-lay
apple compote

coniglio ripieno
koh-nee-lyoh ree-pye-noh
stuffed rabbit

cotoletta d'agnello
koh-toh-layt-ta da-nyel-loh
lamb cutlet

cotoletta di maiale
koh-toh-layt-ta dee ma-yah lay
pork cutlet

cotoletta di vitello
koh-toh-layt-ta dee vee-tel-loh
veal cutlet

cotoletta
koh-toh-layt-ta
plain cutlet

cozze
kots-tsay
mussels

crem caramel
krem ka-ra-mayl
crème caramel

crema di funghi
kre-ma dee foon-ghee
cream of mushroom soup

crescione
cray-shoh-nay
watercress

datteri
dat-tay-ree
dates

dolce di formaggio / ricotta
dohl-chay dee fohr-maj-joh / ree-cot-ta
cheese cake

dolce di mandorle
dohl-chay dee man-dohr-lay
almond cake

dolce di mele
dohl-chay dee may-lay
apple cake

dolce di riso
dohl-chay dee ree-zoh
rice pudding

dolce
dohl-chay
cake

dragoncello
dra-gohn-chel-loh
tarragon

erba cipollina
er-ba chee-pohl-lee-na
chives

fagiano
fa-jah-noh
pheasant

fagioli bianchi
fa-jo-lee byan-kee
broad beans

fagioli
fa-jo-lee
French beans

Menu reader

filetto di merluzzo
*fee-**layt**-toh dee mayr-**loots**-so*
hake fillet

foglia d'alloro
*fo-lya dal-**lo**-roh*
bay leaf

fragole
frah-goh-lay
strawberries

fragole con la panna
*frah-goh-lay kohn la **pan**-na*
strawberries with cream

frittelle
*freet-**tel**-lay*
fritters

frutta con panna montata
*froot-ta kohn **pan**-na mohn-
tah-ta*
fruit with whipped cream

funghi
foon-ghee
mushrooms

funghi con l'aglio
*foon-ghee kohn **la**-lyoh*
mushrooms with garlic

funghi in salsa
*foon-ghee een **sal**-sa*
mushrooms in sauce

gambero di fiume
*gam-bay-roh dee **fyoo**-may*
crayfish

gelato
*jay-**lah**-toh*
ice cream

granturco dolce
*gran-**toor**-koh **dohl**-chay*
sweet corn

. . . in salsa
*. . . een **sal**-sa*
. . . in sauce

indivia
*een-**dee**-vya*
chicory

insalata di cetrioli
*een-sa-**lah**-ta dee
chay-tree-o-lee*
cucumber salad

insalata di patate
*een-sa-**lah**-ta dee pa-**tah**-tay*
potato salad

insalata di pomodori
een-sa-lah-ta dee poh-moh-do-ree
tomato salad

insalata
een-sa-lah-ta
salad

insalata mista
een-sa-lah-ta mee-sta
mixed salad

insalata russa
een-sa-lah-ta roos-sa
Russian salad

lamponi
lam-poh-nee
raspberries

lattuga
lat-too-ga
lettuce

limone
lee-moh-nay
lemon

lingua
leen-gwa
tongue

macedonia di frutta
ma-chay-do-nya dee froot-ta
fruit salad

manzo allo spiedo
man-dzoh al-loh spye-doh
ox on the spit

manzo brasato
man-dzoh bra-zah-toh
braised beef

marmellata
mar-mayl-lah-ta
jam

melanzana
may-lan-dzah-na
aubergine

melanzane alla parmigiana
may-lan-tsah-nay al-la par-mee-jah-na
aubergines with mozzarella, tomato sauce and ham

mele
may-lay
apples

137

Menu reader

melograno
*may-loh-**grah**-noh*
pomegranate

melone
*may-**loh**-nay*
melon

menta
***mayn**-ta*
mint

meringa al limone
*may-**reen**-ga al lee-**moh**-nay*
lemon meringue

minestra di fagioli
*mee-**ne**-stra dee fa-**joh**-lee*
kidney-bean soup

minestra di pollo
*mee-**ne**-stra dee **pohl**-loh*
chicken soup

minestra di pomodoro
*mee-**ne**-stra dee
poh-moh-**do**-roh*
tomato soup

minestra di porri
*mee-**ne**-stra dee **por**-ree*
leek soup

mousse di cioccolata
*moos dee chohk-koh-**lah**-ta*
chocolate mousse

oca
o-ka
goose

olio
o-lyoh
oil

olive
*oh-**lee**-vay*
olives

ostriche
o-stree-kay
oysters

pan di Spagna
*pan dee **spa**-nya*
sponge cake

panini
*pa-**nee**-nee*
bread rolls

panino con il würstel
*pa-**nee**-noh kohn eel **voor**-stayl*
hot dog

passato di verdura
*pas-**sah**-toh dee vayr-**doo**-ra*
cream of vegetable soup

pasta all'uovo
*pa-sta al-**lwo**-voh*
egg noodles

pasta col pesto
*pa-sta kohl **pay**-stoh*
pasta and pesto

pasta e fagioli
*pa-sta ay fa-**joh**-lee*
pasta and beans

pasta
pa-sta
pasta

pasticcio di lasagne
*pa-**stee**-choh dee la-**za**-nyay*
lasagne

pastinaca
*pa-stee-**nah**-ka*
parsnip

patate arroste
*pa-**tah**-tay ar-**ros**-tay*
roast potatoes

patate fritte
*pa-**tah**-tay **freet**-tay*
French fries

peperone rosso
*pay-pay-**roh**-nay **rohs**-soh*
red pepper

peperone verde
*pay-pay-**roh**-nay **vayr**-day*
green pepper

pera
pay-ra
pear

pesca
pe-ska
peach

pesce
pay-shay
fish

pesce marinato
*pay-shay ma-ree-**nah**-toh*
marinated fish

piselli
*pee-**zel**-lee*
peas

Menu reader

pollo al forno / arrosto
*pohl-loh al fohr-noh /
ar-ro-stoh*
baked / roast chicken

pollo impanato
pohl-loh eem-pa-nah-toh
fried/breaded chicken

pomodori
poh-moh-do-ree
tomatoes

pompelmo
pohm-pel-moh
grapefruit

porri
por-ree
leeks

prezzemolo
prayts-say-moh-loh
parsley

prosciutto
proh-shoot-toh
ham

prosciutto crudo
proh-shoot-toh cru-do
smoked ham

prugne
proo-nyay
plums

purè di patate
poo-re dee pa-tah-tay
mashed potatoes

rapa
rah-pa
turnip

ravanelli
ra-va-nel-lee
radishes

ribes
ree-bays
blackcurrants

riso e piselli
ree-zoh ay pee-zel-lee
pea soup

risotto di pesce
ree-zot-toh dee pay-shay
rice and fish

risotto di spinaci
ree-zot-toh dee spee-nah-chee
rice and spinach

risotto di zucchine
ree-zot-toh dee tsoo-kee-nay
rice and courgettes

rognoni trifolati
roh-nyoh-nee tree-foh-lah-tee
stewed kidney

rosmarino
rohz-ma-ree-noh
rosemary

salsa al vino
sal-sa al vee-noh
wine sauce

salsa di cipolle
sal-sa dee chee-pohl-lay
onion sauce

salsa di mele
sal-sa dee may-lay
apple sauce

salsa di peperoni verdi
sal-sa dee pay-pay-roh-nee vayr-dee
green pepper sauce

salsa di pomodoro
sal-sa deepoh-moh-do-ree
tomato sauce

salsiccia
sal-see-cha
sausage

salvia
sal-vya
sage

sandwich di prosciutto
saynd-veech dee proh-shoot-toh
ham sandwich

sandwich freddo
saynd-veech frayd-doh
cold sandwich

sardine
sar-dee-nay
sardines

scalogni
ska-loh-nyee
shallots

scampi
skam-pee
scampi

sedano
se-da-noh
celery

Menu reader

seppia
sayp-pya
cuttlefish

sgombro marinato
sgohm-broh ma-ree-nah-toh
marinated mackerel

sgombro
sgohm-broh
mackerel

spaghetti
spa-gayt-tee
spaghetti

spezzatino di manzo
spayts-sa-tee-noh dee man-dzoh
beef stew

spezzatino di pollo
spayts-sa-tee-noh dee pohl-loh
chicken stew

spinaci
spee-nah-chee
spinach

stinco (d'agnello, ecc.)
steen-koh (da-nyel-loh...)
shank (of lamb, etc)

stufato di fagioli
stoo-fah-toh dee fa-joh-lee
bean stew

susine verdi
soo-zee-nay vayr-dee
greengages

tacchino
tak-kee-noh
turkey

timo
tee-moh
thyme

tonno
tohn-noh
tuna

torta
tohr-ta
pie

trippa
treep-pa
tripe

trota bollita
tro-ta bohl-lee-ta
boiled trout

trota fritta
tro-ta freet-ta
fried trout

trota
tro-ta
trout

uova all'occhio di bue
wo-va-al-lok-kyoh dee boo-ay
fried eggs

uova e pancetta
wo-va ay pan-chayt-ta
eggs with bacon

uova e prosciutto
wo-va ay proh-shoot-toh
eggs with ham

uova strapazzate
wo-va stra-pats-sah-tay
scrambled eggs

uovo alla coque
wo-voh al-la kok
soft boiled egg

uva
oo-va
grapes

verdure
vayr-doo-ray
vegetables

vongole
vohn-goh-lay
clams

yogurt
yo-goort
yoghurt

zucca
tsook-ka
marrow

zucchine
tsook-kee-nay
courgettes

zuppa di pesce
tsoop-pa dee pay-shay
fish soup

Wine

Italy is the world's largest producer of wine. Vines are grown in every province, from the northern Alps right down to southern Sicily. The variety of individual wines produced, and of wine-making methods, is bewildering.

Wine-making methods have undergone something of a revolution in recent years, and Italy is now producing more and more high-quality (and good-value) wines.

Italian red wines are traditionally superior to whites, but with the new high-tech methods and the introduction of French and other foreign grape varieties, more and more good whites are being produced (particularly in the north).

Wine classification

The classification of Italian wines is no real guarantee of quality. Although most of the top names are included in the DOCG or DOC categories, explained below, some of the best wines are categorized as *vini da tavola* because they break the local DOC regulations (and are often better for doing so). Ultimately, the producer's name on the bottle is the only reliable indication of quality.

Denominazione di Origine Controllata e Garantita (DOCG)

Created in 1983 for the theoretically top tier of wines. Rules are supposedly more stringent than those for DOC wines, and wines are tasted by special panel of experts. The first five wines to be given the classification rate among Italy's great wines: Barolo, Barbaresco. Brunello di Montalcino, Vino Nobile di Montepulciano and Chianti. Nine other wines have been added since.

Denominazione di Origine Controllata
A guarantee of origin, but not necessarily of quality, covering over 700 wines from 250 different zones.

Vino da Tavola con Indicazione Geografica
Gives some indication of place of origin and perhaps grape type. Similar to the French *Vin de Pays*.

Vino da Tavola
Basic wines and (just to confuse you) good ones that defy local regulations.

Wine vocabulary

abboccato – medium-sweet wine
amabile – sweet
annata – vintage (year)
azienda agricola – estate that makes and bottles its own wine
bianco – white
bicchiere – glass
bottiglia – bottle

Wine vocabulary

cantina – wine cellar or winery

caraffa – carafe

cascina – wine farm or estate

classico – from the heart of a particular area (for a DOC wine)

consorzio – marketing consortium

cooperativa – wine growers' cooperative

degustazione – wine tasting

dolce – sweet

enoteca – wine library (often a place where you can taste and buy wines)

etichetta – label

fattoria – wine-growing farm or estate

frizzante – slightly sparkling

leggero – light

metodo champenois or *metodo classico* – champagne method of making sparkling wine

pieno – full-bodied

produttore – producer

riserva – applied to DOC or DOCG wines that have undergone extra aging – not always a good thing

rosato – rosé

rosso – red

secco – dry

spumante – sparkling

superiore – DOC wine with more alcohol longer aging, etc, but not necessarily superior quality

tenuta – estate
uva – grape
vendemmia – grape harvest (also used for vintage)
vigna – vineyard
vite – vine

Wine regions

The northwest

Italy's best known wine-growing region, which owes its fame to the great reds of Piedmont. The tough and tannic Nebbiolo grape-maker of Barolo, Barberesco and other big reds is the dominant grape, but the robust Barbera accounts for over half the region's red wines. Another important grape is the Dolcetto, producing fresh fruitier wines. White wine is not big business apart from the (frequently underrated) sparkling Asti Spumante and Moscato d'Asti, both made from the Moscato grape. The main still white is the dry light Cortese. Piedmont is well organised for wine touring.

Wine production in the Valle d'Aosta and Liguria is modest by comparison and most is kept for home consumption.

The northeast

An innovative, efficiently run region producing some excellent light fruity wines.

Alto Adige/Sud-Tirol – a beautiful mountainous region where German is widely spoken and vineyards are tended with

Wine regions

Austrian precision. There are more and more high-quality whites, including oak-aged Chardonnays. The majority of wines are red, based on the Schiava (or Vernatsch) grape, which can produce excellent light reds. Lagrein makes dark, really flavourful reds and dry rosés.

Trentino – south of Alto Adige and far more Italian in character. With the exception of wines from the Pinot Bianco and Chardonnay grapes grown north of Trento, standards are generally lower.

Veneto – the producer of more wine than any other region of Italy. The bulk is made up of the light refreshing and undemanding Soave, Valpolicella and Bardolino. Look for the rich but austere Recioto della Valpolicella.

Friuli-Venezia Giulia the producer of unmistakably fruity wines. Tocai is the local favourite. The famous Picolit, a rich, sweet dessert wine, is now outclassed by the sensational Ramandolo di Verduzzo.

Emilia-Romagna – a major producer of the *frizzante* Lambrusco, mostly dismissed by connoisseurs as 'alcoholic pop' but locally often delicious – red and white, sweet and dry.

Lombardy – an underrated wine area. Best are the reds from the Valtellina and the Oltrepò Pavese zone in the Po valley.

The centre

An area of remarkably diverse wines, including the familiar names of Frascati, Chianti and Orvieto.

Tuscany – a beautiful region for wine touring and home of Italy's most famous wine. Chianti varies from the sharp young reds (traditionally sold in the round straw-covered *fiaschi*) to the deep-coloured, estate-bottled, barrel-aged reds that come in claret-shaped bottles.

Chianti is divided into seven regions, most important of which are Chianti Classico, Rufina, Colli Fiorentini and Colli Senesi. Classicos are usually denoted by a black cockerel symbol; non-Classico Chiantis sometimes carry a cherub (*putto*) seal on the neck label.

The most distinguished non-Chianti reds are the Vino Nobile di Montepulciano, the powerful and phenomenally expensive Brunello di Montalcino and the smooth and fragrant Carmignano. The dry Vernaccia di San Gimignano is traditionally the best white wine – and at its best still is.

Umbria – famous for Orvieto, historically semi-sweet, now mostly dry.

Lazio – the wine region of Rome, producing the commercial Frascati and the notoriously named Est! Est!! Est!!!

Marche and *Abruzzo* – the reliable light, dry Verdicchio is the main wine of Marche. In Abruzzo the Montepulciano grape produces the consistently good, reasonably priced Montepulciano d'Abruzzo (not to be confused with Vino Nobile di Montepulciano).

The south and the islands

These areas produce huge quantities of wine, much of it exported for blending. Quality has improved with the modernisation of methods, Sicily making the greatest advance.

On the mainland, Apulia is the main wine-making area,

producing dark, strong cutting wines, many of which are added to frail pale wines of the north. In Basilicata, the rare, thickly flavoured Aglianico del Vulture can be outstanding.

Drinks reader

acqua minerale
*ak-kwa mee-nay-**rah**-lay*
mineral water

acqua tonica
ak-kwa to-nee-ka
tonic water

aranciata
*a-ran-**chah**-ta*
orange drink

birra
beer-ra
beer

birra forte
beer-ra fohr-tay
stout

birra in bottiglia
*beer-ra een boht-**tee**-lya*
bottled beer

birra in lattina
*beer-ra een lat-**tee**-na*
canned beer

caffè col latte
*kaf-fe kohl **lat**-tay*
coffee with milk

caffè decaffeinato
*kaf-fe day-kaf-fay-ee-**nah**-toh*
decaffeinated coffee

caffè freddo
*kaf-fe **frayd**-doh*
iced coffee

caffè
kaf-fe
coffee

caffè solubile
*kaf-fe soh-**loo**-bee-lay*
instant coffee

camomilla
*ka-moh-**meel**-la*
camomile tea

cappuccino
*kap-poo-**chee**-noh*
cappuccino

champagne
*sham-**pan***
champagne

coca-cola
*ko-ka **ko**-la*
coke

grappa di mele
*grap-pa dee **may**-lay*
apple brandy

limonata
*lee-moh-**nah**-ta*
lemonade

liquore
*lee-**kwoh**-ray*
liqueur

rum
room
rum

selz
selts
soda

sidro
see-droh
cider

succo d'arancia
*sook-koh da-**ran**-cha*
orange juice

succo d'uva
*sook-koh **doo**-va*
grape juice

succo di albicocca
*sook-koh dee al-bee-**kok**-ka*
apricot juice

succo di mela
*sook-koh dee **may**-la*
apple juice

succo di pesca
*sook-koh dee **pe**-ska*
peach juice

tè al limone
*te al lee-**moh**-nay*
lemon tea

Drinks reader

tè col latte
te kohl lat-tay
tea with milk

un brandy
oon brayn-dee
a brandy

una birra grande
oo-na beer-ra gran-day
a large beer

vermut
vayr-moot
vermouth

vino rosato
vee-noh roh-zah-toh
rosé wine

whisky
wee-skee
whisky

OUT AND ABOUT

The weather

There is much regional variation in the weather. Two winds, in particular, can affect temperatures – the cold *bora* across northern Italy at the beginning of the year and the hot, heavy *scirocco*, blowing up from the south in the summer.

Is it going to get any warmer?
Farà più caldo?
*fa-**ra** pyoo **kal**-doh*

Is it going to stay like this?
Resterà così?
*ray-stay-**ra** coh-**zee***

Is there going to be a thunderstorm?
Ci sarà un temporale?
*chee sa-**ra** oon taym-poh-**rah**-lay*

Isn't it a lovely day?
Che bella giornata!
*kay **bel**-la johr-**nah**-ta*

It has stopped snowing
Ha smesso di nevicare
*a **zmays**-soh dee nay-vee-**kah**-ray*

The weather

It is far too hot
Fa troppo caldo
*fa **trop**-poh **kal**-doh*

It is foggy
C'è nebbia
*che **nayb**-bya*

It is raining again
Piove di nuovo
***pyo**-vay dee **nwo**-voh*

It is very cold
Fa molto freddo
*fa **mohl**-toh **frayd**-doh*

It is very windy
C'è molto vento
*che **mohl**-toh **ven**-toh*

It is a very clear night
E' una notte molto chiara
*e **oo**-na **not**-tay **mohl**-toh **kyah**-ra*

There is a cool breeze
C'è un'arietta fresca
*che oo-na-**ryayt**-ta **fray**-ska*

It is going to be fine
Farà bel tempo
*fa-**ra** bel **tem**-poh*

Is it going to be windy?
Ci sarà vento?
*chee sa-**ra ven**-toh*

Is it going to rain?
Pioverà?
*pyoh-vay-**ra***

Is it going to snow
Nevicherà?
*nay-vee-kay-**ra***

What is the temperature?
Quanti gradi sono?
*kwan-tee **grah**-dee soh-noh*

Will the weather improve?
Il tempo migliorerà?
*eel **tem**-poh mee-lyoh-ray-**ra***

Will the wind die down?
Cesserà il vento?
*chays-say-**ra** eel **ven**-toh*

Will it be cold tonight?
Farà freddo stanotte?
*fa-**ra frayd**-doh sta-**not**-tay*

On the beach

Despite its 8,000 kilometres of coastline, Italy is not liberally endowed with beautiful sandy beaches. Where they exist, they have often been spoilt by tourist development or they are so remote you need a boat to get to them. Of course there are exceptions, but the chic resorts with the beautiful beaches and scenery are beyond most people's budgets.

Beaches are usually divided up into private concession areas, distinguished by their regimented rows of brightly coloured parasols. Here you pay for the use of facilities, which usually include changing cabins, showers and sunbeds. Prices usually vary from concession to concession along the same beach, so it's worth finding out prices first. Rates are cheaper out of high season and for weekly or fortnightly bookings. Italian beaches are always packed in summer so book your place as soon as you arrive. If you don't want to pay you have to use the less desirable public beaches, few of which have any facilities.

Most seaside regions offer a choice of watersports, including windsurfing, pedaloes, rowing boats and sailing. The best facilities are along the Adriatic coast.

Can you recommend a quiet beach?
Mi può consigliare una spiaggia?
*mee pwo kohn-see-**lyah**-ray **oo**-na **spyaj**-ja*

On the beach

Is it possible — to go sailing?
Si può — fare della vela?
*see pwo — **fah**-ray **del**-la a **vay**-la*

> **— to go surfing?**
> — fare del surf?
> *— **fah**-ray dayl soorf*

> **— to go water-skiing?**
> — fare dello sci d'acqua?
> *— **fah**-ray **dayl**-loh shee **dak**-kwa*

> **— to go windsurfing?**
> — fare dello wind surf?
> *— **fah**-ray **dayl**-loh weend soorf*

Can we change here?
Possiamo cambiarci qui?
*pohs-**syah**-moh kam-**byahr**-chee kwee*

Is it safe to swim here?
E' pericoloso nuotare qui?
*e pay-ree-koh-**loh**-zoh nwoh-**tah**-ray kwee*

Is the current strong?
E' forte la corrente?
*e **fohr**-tay la kohr-**ren**-tay*

Is the sea calm?
E' calmo il mare?
*e **kal**-moh eel **mah**-ray*

Is the water warm?
E' calda l'acqua?
e kal-da lak-kw

Is there a lifeguard here?
C'è un bagnino qui?
che oon ba-nyee-noh kwee

Is this beach private?
E' una spiaggia privata?
e oo-na spyaj-ja pree-vah-ta

When is — high tide?
A che ora è — l'alta marea?
a kay oh-ra e — lal-ta ma-ray-a

— low tide?
— la bassa marea?
— la bas-sa ma-ray-a

Sport and recreation

Is there a heated swimming pool?
C'è una piscina riscaldata?
che oo-na pee-shee-na ree-skal-dah-t

Can I rent — a sailing boat?
Possiamo affittare — una barca a vela?
pohs-syah-moh af-feet-tah-ray — oo-na bahr-ka a vay-la

Sport and recreation

> **— a rowing boat?**
> — una barca a remi?
> — *oo-na **bahr**-ka a **ray**-mee*

Can I rent the equipment?
Posso affittare l'equipaggiamento?
*pos-soh af-feet-**tah**-ray lay-kwee-paj-ja-**mayn**-toh*

Do I have to pay a deposit?
Devo pagare un deposito?
***day**-voh pa-**gah**-ray oon day-**po**-zee-toh*

> **Can we play — tennis?**
> Si può giocare — a tennis?
> *see pwo joh-**kah**-ray — a **ten**-nees*

> **— golf?**
> — a golf?
> — *a golf*

> **— volleyball?**
> — a pallavolo?
> — *a pal-la-**voh**-loh*

Can we go riding?
Si può andare a cavallo?
*see pwo an-**da**-ray a ka-**val**-loh*

Where can we fish?
Dove si può pescare?
***doh**-vay see pwo pay-**skah**-ray*

Do we need a permit?
C'è bisogno di un permesso?
che bee-zoh-nyoh dee oon payr-mays-so

Entertainment

Is there — a disco?
    C'è — una discoteca?
    che — oo-na dee-skoh-te-ka

        — a good nightclub?
        — un buon night?
        — oon bwon na-eet

        — a theatre?
        — un teatro?
        — oon tay-ah-troh

How much is it per person?
Quanto costa a persona?
kwan-toh coh-sta a payr-soh-na

How much is it to get in?
Quanto costa l'entrata?
kwan-toh coh-sta layn-trah-ta

Is there a reduction for children?
C'è uno sconto per i bambini?
che oo-noh skohn-toh payr ee bam-bee-nee

Museums and galleries

Two stall tickets, please
Due biglietti in platea, per favore
***doo**-ay bee-**lyayt**-tee een pla-**te**-a, payr fa-**voh**-ray*

Two tickets, please
Due biglietti, per favore
***doo**-ay bee-**lyayt**-tee, payr fa-**voh**-ray*

Are there any films in English?
Ci sono film in inglese?
*chee **soh**-noh feelm een een-**glay**-zay*

Museums and galleries

Although Florence, Rome and Venice are undisputably the richest repositories of art in Italy, nearly every little town seems to have an art gallery, often in an old *palazzo* or in the town hall, containing at least one or two masterpieces.

While gallery-gazing can be the most rewarding experience of a visit to Italy, it can also be the most frustrating. Opening hours change frequently, museums are frequently closed for restoration or lack of staff, and the crowding in the top sights of tourist cities can be very uncomfortable. Opening hours vary between regions and with the season, but as a general rule state museums are open from 9.00am to 2.00pm, and on Sundays from 9.00am to 1.00pm. Museums are usually shut for at least one day of the week – usually Monday.

Sightseeing

Are there any boat trips on the river?
Ci sono gite in barca sul fiume?
chee soh-noh jee-tay een bahr-ka sool fyoo-may

Are there any guided tours of the castle?
Ci sono visite guidate al castello?
chee soh-noh vee-zee-tay gwee-dah-tay al ka-stel-loh

Are there any guided tours?
Ci sono visite guidate?
chee soh-noh vee-zee-tay gwee-dah-tay

Is there a tour of the cathedral?
C'è una visita alla cattedrale?
che oo-na vee-zee-ta al-la kat-tay-drah-lay

When is the bus tour?
A che ora è il giro in pullman?
a kay oh-ra e eel jee-roh een pool-man

How long does the tour take?
Quanto dura il giro?
kwan-toh doo-ra eel jee-roh

What is there to see here?
Che cosa c'è da vedere qui?
kay co-za che da vay-day-ray kwee

161

Sightseeing

What is this building?
Che cos'è quest'edificio?
kay co-ze kwe-stay-dee-fee-choh

When was it built?
Quando è stato costruito?
kwan-doh e stah-toh koh-stroo-ee-toh

Is it open to the public?
E' aperto al pubblico?
e a-per-toh al poob-blee-koh

Can we go in?
Possiamo entrare?
pohs-syah-moh ayn-trah-ray

What is the admission charge?
Quant'è l'entrata?
kwan-te layn-trah-ta

How much is it for a child?
Quanto costa il biglietto per un bambino?
kwan-toh coh-sta eel bee-lyayt-toh payr oon bam-bee-noh

Can we go up to the top?
Possiamo andare fino in cima?
poh-syah-moh an-dah-ray fee-noh een chee-ma

Is this the best view?
Questa è la vista migliore?
kwe-sta e la vee-sta mee-lyoh-ray

Have you got an English guidebook?
Avete una guida in inglese?
a-vay-tay oo-na gwee-da een een-glay-zay

Is there a guide book?
C'è una guida?
che oo-na gwee-da

Is there an English-speaking guide?
C'è una guida che parla inglese?
che oo-na gwee-da kay pahr-la een-glay-zay

What time does the gallery open?
A che ora apre la galleria?
a kay oh-ra ah-pray la gal-lay-ree-a

Can I take photos?
Posso fare delle fotografie?
pos-soh fah-ray dayl-lay foh-toh-gra-fee-ay

Can I use flash?
Posso usare il flash?
pos-soh oo-zah-ray eel flesh

Souvenirs

Where can I buy postcards?
Dove posso comprare delle cartoline?
doh-vay pos-soh kohm-prah-ray dayl-lay kar-toh-lee-nay

Going to church

I am looking for a souvenir
Cerco un souvenir
*chayr-koh oon soov-**neer***

Where can we buy souvenirs?
Dove possiamo comprare dei souvenir?
*doh-vay pohs-**syah**-moh kohm-**prah**-ray **day**-ee soov-**neer***

Have you got any colour slides?
Avete diapositive a colori?
*a-**vay**-tay dee-a-poh-zee-**tee**-vay a koh-**loh**-ree*

Going to church

When visiting a church, dress appropriately. Do not wear shorts or short skirts and women should ensure that their shoulders are covered. If you are just sightseeing then it is advisable to arrange to visit when there is not a religious service in progress.

> **I would like to see — a priest**
> Vorrei parlare con — un sacerdote
> *vor-**re**-ee par-**lah**-ray kohn — oon sa-chayr-**do**-tay*

> **— a minister**
> — un pastore
> — *oon pa-**stoh**-ray*

> **— a rabbi**
> — un rabbino
> — *oon rab-**bee**-noh*

Where is the — Catholic church?
  Dov'è la — chiesa cattolica?
  doh-ve la — kye-za kat-tol-lee-ka

  — Baptist church?
  — chiesa battista?
  — *kye-za bat-tee-sta*

  — mosque?
  — moschea?
  — *moh-ske-a*

  — Protestant church?
  — chiesa protestante?
  — *kye-za proh-tay-stan-tay*

  — synagogue?
  — sinagoga ?
  — *see-na-go-ga*

What time is the service?
A che ora è la funzione?
a kay oh-ra e la foon-tsyoh-nay

Shopping

For many foreigners, shopping forms a crucial part of any trip to Italy. Though bargains are few and far between these days, Italian craftsmanship and style still flourish. Even in the humblest back streets you can come across beautifully made clothes, leather goods and ceramics.

Best buys

The beautifully made clothes and shoes to be found in Italy are difficult to resist. But prices can be prohibitive, particularly in the chic boutiques of the cities, with top designer names. For more down-to-earth prices (and goods) try the chain stores downmarket UPIM, mid-range Standa and slightly more stylish La Rinascente.

Many traditional crafts survive in Italy, with different regional specialities. (The regions given in brackets below are notable sources, but not the only ones.)

Ceramics (Véneto, Tuscany, Umbria, the south) – brightly coloured glazed earthenware and hand-painted pots are good value.

Glass (Venice area, especially Murano) – the centuries-old tradition of coloured glass goes on – and adapts to modern times with trendy designs.

Lace (Venice area, especially Burano) – hand-made lace is cheaper than in the UK, but watch out for imitations from the East.

Leather (Florence area) – top-quality leather goods are very expensive but you can often find reasonably priced wallets, gloves, belts and handbags.

Silk (Milan and Como) – not always cheaper than in the UK.

Opening times

Shops are usually open in the morning from 8.30am or 9.00am to around 1.00pm. In summer, shops in many places then stay closed during the afternoon until 3.30pm, when they reopen for an evening session ending at 7.30 or 8.00pm. In winter they may open earlier – and there are variations in northern Italy, particularly the big cities, where the lunch break is shorter and shops close earlier.

Markets

Almost every town has its weekly market, a colourful and lively affair whose range and quality of fresh produce put English markets to shame: plump peaches, gleaming artichokes and many delicious cooked meats, sausages and patés – ideal for a picnic. The bigger markets also sell clothes, shoes, leather goods and silk: they can be a good

General phrases and requests

source of cheap wool or angora sweaters and other informal wear; though a lot of the goods are merely shoddy.

Markets usually start very early in the morning and finish by about noon.

General phrases and requests

How much is this?
Quanto costa questo?
kwan-toh koh-sta kwe-stoh

How much does that cost?
Quanto costa?
kwan-toh koh-sta

Have you got anything cheaper?
Non avete niente di meno caro?
nohn a-vay-tay nyen-tay dee may-noh kah-roh

How much is it — per kilo?
Quanto costa — al chilo?
kwan-toh koh-sta — al kee-loh

— per metre?
— al metro?
— al may-troh

I like this one
Questo mi piace
kwe-stoh mee pyah-chay

General phrases and requests

I do not like it
Non mi piace
*nohn mee **pyah**-chay*

I will take that one
Prendo quello
***prayn**-doh **kwayl**-loh*

I will take the other one
Prendo quell'altro
***prayn**-doh kwayl-**lal**-troh*

I will take this one
Prendo questo
***prayn**-doh **kwe**-stoh*

No, the other one
No, l'altro
*no, **lal**-troh*

Can I see that one over there?
Posso vedere quella là
***pos**-soh vay-**day**-ray **kwayl**-la la*

Can I see that umbrella?
Posso vedere quell'ombrello?
***pos**-soh vay-**day**-ray kwayl-lohm-**brel**-loh*

Do you sell sunglasses?
Vendete occhiali da sole?
*vayn-**day**-tay ok-**kyah**-lee da **soh**-lay*

General phrases and requests

Can you deliver to my hotel?
Lo può consegnare al mio albergo?
loh pwo kohn-say-nyah-ray al mee-oh al-ber-goh

Can I have a carrier bag?
Posso avere una borsa?
pos-soh a-vay-ray oo-na bohr-sa

Please wrap it up for me
Per favore, me lo incarti
payr fa-voh-ray, may loh een-kar-tee

There is no need to wrap it
Non c'è bisogno che lo incarti
nohn che bee-zoh-nyoh kay loh een-kar-tee

What is the total?
Quant'è in tutto?
kwan-te een toot-toh

Can I have a receipt?
Posso avere una ricevuta?
pos-soh a-vay-ray oo-na ree-chay-voo-ta

Can I have an itemised bill?
Posso avere il conto dettagliato?
pos-soh a-vay-ray eel kohn-toh dayt-ta-lyah-toh

I would like to pay with my credit card
Vorrei pagare con la carta di credito
vor-re-ee pa-gah-ray kohn la kar-ta dee kray-dee-toh

170

General phrases and requests

I do not have enough money
Non ho abbastanza soldi
*nohn oh ab-ba-**stan**-tsa **sol**-de*

You have given me the wrong change
Mi ha dato il resto sbagliato
*mee a **dah**-toh eel **re**-stoh sba-**lyah**-toh*

Will you send it by air freight?
Lo spedirà via aerea?
*loh spay-dee-**ra** vee-a a-e-ray-a*

Can I pay for air insurance?
Posso pagare l'assicurazione per l'aereo?
***pos**-soh pa-**gah**-ray las-see-koo-ra-**tsyoh**-nay payr
 la-**e**-ray-oh*

Please pack it for shipment
Per favore, me lo imballi per la spedizione via mare
*payr fa-**voh**-ray, may loh eem-**bal**-lee payr la
 spay-dee-**tsyoh**-nay **vee**-a **mah**-ray*

We need to buy some food
Dobbiamo comprare da mangiare
*dohb-**byah**-moh kohm-**prah**-ray da man-**jah**-ray*

Where can I buy cassette tapes and compact discs?
Dove posso comprare dei nastri e dei compact?
***doh**-vay **pos**-soh kohm-**prah**-ray **day**-ee **na**-stree ay **day**-ee
 kohm-pakt*

Groceries

Where can I buy some clothes?
Dove posso comprare dei vestiti?
doh-vay pos-soh kohm-prah-ray day-ee vay-stee-tee

Where can I buy tapes for my camcorder?
Dove posso comprare le cassette per la videocamera?
doh-vay pos-soh kohm-prah-ray lay kas-sayt-tay payr la vee-day-oh-ka-may-ra

Where can I get my camcorder repaired?
Dove posso far riparare la mia videocamera?
doh-vay pos-soh fahr ree-pa-rah-ray la mee-a vee-day-oh-ka-may-ra

Where is — the children's department?
   Dov'è — il reparto bambini?
   doh-ve — eel ray-pahr-toh bam-bee-nee

   — the food department?
   — il reparto alimentari?
   — *eel ray-pahr-toh a-lee-mayn-tah-ree*

Food

Supermarkets have not made the impact in Italy that they have in the UK. Traditional food shops and markets will be found in most town centres; the produce will be fresh and will usually reflect the regional cuisine.

Specialist food shops

Salumeria – the equivalent of a delicatessen selling ham, sausages, other cold meats, cheese and often a variety of ready-made dishes such as salads, pasta and pies.

Alimentari – small grocery shop selling basic provisions and a limited selection of vegetables and fruit.

Panificio or *Panetteria* – bakery where fresh bread and rolls (in the past nearly always white, but now increasingly varied, at least in the cities) are often cooked on the premises. Some bakeries also sell slices of cooked pizza, cakes, pastries and hot brioche.

Pasticceria – cake shop, the equivalent of a French patisserie selling pastries, fruit tarts, rich cakes. home-made biscuits, chocolates and so on.

Macelleria – butcher's shop, where meat is priced on the quality of the cut. It's advisable to tell the butcher what you are going to cook and he will give you the appropriate cut. Chickens and rabbits are often sold in other shops.

Supermercato – supermarket. All towns have at least one supermarket. Shopping here is not as much fun as in the small specialised shops or in the markets but they are a way of overcoming the language barrier

Other shops you may come across are: *casa del formaggio* (cheese shop); *latteria* (dairy); *fruttivendolo* (greengrocer); *pescheria* (fish shop); *gelaterla* (ice-cream shop).

Buying groceries

Can I have — a bottle of wine, please?
 Mi dà — una bottiglia di vino, per piacere?
 mee da — ***oo***-*na boht-****tee***-*lya dee* ***vee***-*noh, payr pya-****chay***-*ray*

> **—a kilo of sausages, please?**
> —un chilo di salsicce, per piacere?
> —*oon* ***kee***-*loh dee sal-****see***-*chay, payr pya-****chay***-*ray*

> **—a leg of lamb, please?**
> —una coscia di agnello, per piacere?
> —***oo***-*na* ***ko***-*sha dee a-****nyel***-*loh, payr pya-****chay***-*ray*

> **—a litre of milk, please?**
> —un litro di latte, per piacere?
> —*oon* ***lee***-*troh dee* ***lat***-*tay, payr pya-****chay***-*ray*

> **—some sugar, please?**
> —dello zucchero, per piacere?
> —***dayl***-*loh* ***tsook***-*kay-roh, payr pya-****chay***-*ray*

> **—two steaks, please?**
> —due bistecche, per piacere?
> —***doo***-*ay bee-****stayk***-*kay, payr pya-****chay***-*ray*

I would like — 5 slices of ham
 Vorrei — cinque fette di prosciutto
 *vor-****re***-*ee —* ***cheen***-*kway* ***fayt***-*tay dee proh-****shoot***-*toh*

— **100 g of ground coffee**
— un etto di caffè macinato
— *oon **et**-toh dee kaf-**fe** ma-chee-**nah**-toh*

I would like — **a piece of chocolate**
Vorrei — un pezzo di cioccolato
*vor-**re**-ee* — *oon **pets**-soh dee chohk-koh-**lah**-to*

— **a kilo of potatoes**
— un chilo di patate
— *oon **kee**-loh dee pa-**tah**-tay*

— **half a dozen eggs**
— sei uova
— *se-ee **wo**-va*

— **half a kilo of butter**
— mezzo chilo di burro
— ***med**-zoh **kee**-loh dee **boor**-roh*

Groceries

baby food
mangiare per i bambini
*man-**jah**-ray payr ee
  bam-**bee**-nee*

biscuits
biscotti
*bee-**skot**-tee*

bread
pane
***pah**-nay*

butter
burro
***boor**-roh*

Groceries

cheese
formaggio
*fohr-**maj**-joh*

coffee
caffè
*kaf-**fe***

cream
panna
***pan**-na*

eggs
uova
***wo**-va*

flour
farina
*fa-**ree**-na*

ice cream
gelato
*jay-**lah**-toh*

groceries
generi di drogheria
***jay**-nay-ree dee droh-gay-**ree**-a*

jam
marmellata
*mar-mayl-**lah**-ta*

margarine
margarina
*mar-ga-**ree**-na*

milk
latte
***lat**-tay*

mustard
senape
***se**-na-pay*

oil
olio
***o**-lyoh*

pepper
pepe
***pay**-pay*

rice
riso
***ree**-zoh*

salt
sale
***sah**-lay*

soup
minestra
*mee-**ne**-stra*

sugar
zucchero
tsook-kay-roh

vinegar
aceto
a-chay-toh

tea
tè
te

yoghurt
yogurt
yo-goort

Meat and fish

beef
manzo
man-dzoh

ham
prosciutto
proh-shoot-toh

chicken
pollo
pohl-loh

herring
aringa
a-reen-ga

cod
merluzzo
mayr-loots-soh

kidneys
rognoni
roh-nyoh-nee

fish
pesce
pay-shay

lamb
agnello
a-nyel-loh

hake
merluzzo
mayr-loots-soh

liver
fegato
fay-ga-toh

At the newsagent's

meat
carne
kar-nay

sausages
salsiccia
sal-see-cha

mussels
cozze
kots-say

sole
sogliola
so-lyoh-la

pork
maiale
ma-yah-lay

veal
vitello
vee-tel-loh

At the newsagent's

Do you have — English books?
Avete dei — libri in inglese?
a-vay-tay day-ee — lee-bree een een-glay-zay

— English newspapers?
— giornali inglesi?
— johr-nah-lee een-glay-zee

Do you have postcards?
Avete delle cartoline?
a-vay-tay dayl-lay kar-toh-lee-nay

Do you sell — English paperbacks?
Vendete — tascabili in inglese?
vayn-day-tay — tas-ka-beel-ee een een-glay-zay

— **street maps?**
— carte stradali?
— ***kar**-tay stra-**dah**-lee*

— **coloured pencils?**
— matite colorate?
— ma-**tee**-tay koh-loh-**rah**-tay

— **drawing paper?**
— carta da disegno?
— **kar**-ta da dee-**zay**-nyoh

— **felt pens?**
— pennarelli?
— payn-na-**rel**-lee

I need — some note paper
Ho bisogno — di carta da lettere
*oh bee-**zoh**-nyoh — dee **kar**-ta da **let**-tay-ray*

— **some adhesive tape**
— nastro adesivo
— **na**-stroh a-day-**zee**-voh

— **some envelopes**
— buste
— **boo**-stay

— **a bottle of ink**
— una bottiglietta d'inchiostro
— ***oo**-na boht-tee-**lyayt**-ta deen-**kyo**-stroh*

179

At the tobacconist's

—— **a pen**
—— una penna
—— **oo**-na **payn**-na

—— **a pencil**
—— una matita
—— **oo**-na ma-**tee**-ta

—— **a local map**
—— carte della città
—— **kar**-tay **dayl**-la cheet-**ta**

—— **a road map**
—— carte stradali
—— **kar**-tay stra-**dah**-lee

At the tobacconist's

Do you have —— cigarette papers?
   Avete —— carta per sigarette?
*a-**vay**-tay —— **kar**-ta payr see-ga-**rayt**-tay*

—— **box of matches?**
—— una scatola di fiammiferi?
—— *oo-na **skah**-toh-la dee fyam-**mee**-fay-ree*

—— **a cigar?**
—— un sigaro?
—— *oon **see**-ga-roh*

180

At the tobacconist's

— a cigarette lighter?
— un accendino?
— *oon a-chayn-dee-noh*

— a gas (butane) refill?
— una bomboletta di gas
— *oo-na bohm-boh-layt-ta dee gas*

— a pouch of pipe tobacco?
— una busta di tabacco da pipa?
— *oo-na boo-sta dee ta-bak-koh da pee-pa*

— pipe cleaners?
— pulitori per pipa?
— *poo-lee-toh-ree payr pee-pa*

— rolling tobacco?
— tabacco per sigarette?
— *ta-bak-koh payr see-ga-rayt-tay*

A packet of . . . please
Un pacchetto di . . . per piacere
oon pak-kayt-toh dee . . . payr pya-chay-ray

— with filter tips
— con filtro
— *kohn feel-troh*

— without filters
— senza filtro
— *sen-tsa feel-troh*

At the chemist's

Have you got any English brands?
Avete sigarette inglesi?
*a-**vay**-tay see-ga-**rayt**-tay een-**glay**-zee*

At the chemist's

I need some high-protection suntan cream
Ho bisogno di una crema solare ad alta protezione
*oh bee-**zoh**-nyoh dee **oo**-na **kray**-ma soh-**lah**-ray ad **al**-ta proh-tay-**tsyoh**-nay*

Do you have toothpaste?
Avete del dentifricio
*a-**vay**-tay dayl dayn-tee-**free**-choh*

Can you give me something for insect bites?
Mi può dare qualche cosa per le punture d'insetto?
*mee pwo **dah**-ray **kwal**-kay **ko**-za payr lay poon-**too**-ray deen-**sayt**-toh*

Can you give me something for a headache?
Mi può dare qualche cosa per il mal di testa?
*mee pwo **dah**-ray **kwal**-kay **ko**-za payr eel mal dee **te**-sta*

Can you give me something for toothache?
Mi può dare qualche cosa per il mal di denti?
*mee pwo **dah**-ray **kwal**-kay **ko**-za payr eel mal dee **den**-tee*

Can you give me something for a cold?
Mi può dare qualche cosa per il raffreddore?
*mee pwo **dah**-ray **kwal**-kay **ko**-za payr eel raf-frayd-**doh**-ray*

At the chemist's

Can you give me something for a cough?
Mi può dare qualche cosa per la tosse?
*mee pwo **dah**-ray **kwal**-kay **ko**-za payr la **tohs**-say*

Can you give me something for a sore throat?
Mi può dare qualche cosa per il mal di gola?
*mee pwo **dah**-ray **kwal**-kay **ko**-za payr eel mal dee **goh**-la*

Can you give me something for an upset stomach?
Mi può dare qualche cosa per il mal di stomaco?
*mee pwo **dah**-ray **kwal**-kay **ko**-za payr eel mal dee **sto**-ma-koh*

Can you give me something for chapped lips?
Mi può dare qualche cosa per le labbra screpolate?
*mee pwo **dah**-ray **kwal**-kay **ko**-za payr lay **lab**-bra skray-
poh-**lah**-tay*

Can you give me something for hay fever?
Mi può dare qualche cosa per il raffreddore del fieno?
*mee pwo **dah**-ray **kwal**-kay **ko**-za payr eel raf-frayd-**doh**-ray
dayl **fye**-noh*

Can you give me something for sunburn?
Mi può dare qualche cosa per una bruciatura da sole?
*mee pwo **dah**-ray **kwal**-kay **ko**-za payr oo-na broo-cha-**too**-ra
da **soh**-lay*

Do I need a prescription?
C'è bisogno della ricetta?
*che bee-**zoh**-nyoh day-la ree-**chet**-ta*

Medicines and toiletries

How many do I take?
Quante ne prendo?
*kwan-tay nay **prayn**-doh*

How often do I take them?
Ogni quanto le prendo?
***oh**-nyee **kwan**-toh lay **prayn**-doh*

Are they safe for children to take?
Possono prenderle i bambini?
***pohs**-soh-noh **prayn**-dayr-lay ee bam-**bee**-nee*

Medicines and toiletries

aftershave
dopobarba
*doh-poh-**bar**-ba*

antihistamine
antistaminico
*an-tee-sta-**mee**-nee-koh*

antiseptic
disinfettante
*dee-zeen-fayt-**tan**-tay*

aspirin
aspirina
*as-pee-**ree**-na*

band-aid
cerotto
*chay-**rot**-toh*

bandage
garza
***gar**-dza*

bath salts
sali da bagno
***sah**-lee da **ba**-nyoh*

bubble bath
bagno di schiuma
***ba**-nyoh dee **skyoo**-ma*

Medicines and toiletries

cleansing milk
latte detergente
lat-tay day-tayr-jen-tay

contraceptive
contracettivo
kohn-tra-chayt-tee-voh

cotton wool
cotone idrofilo
koh-toh-nay i-dro-fee-loh

deodorant
deodorante
day-oh-doh-ran-tay

disinfectant
disinfettante
dee-zeen-fayt-tan-tay

eau de Cologne
acqua di Colonia
ak-kwa dee koh-lo-nya

eye shadow
trucco per gli occhi
trook-koh payr lyee ok-kee

hair spray
lacca
lak-ka

hand cream
crema per le mani
kray-ma payr lay mah-nee

insect repellent
antinsetti
an-teen-sayt-tee

laxative
purgante / lassativo
poor-gan-tay / la-sa-tee-vo

lipstick
rossetto
rohs-sayt-toh

mascara
rimmel
reem-mayl

mouthwash
collutorio
ko-loo-toh-ree-oo

nail file
lima per le unghie
lee-ma payr lay oon-gyay

nail varnish remover
acetone
a-chay-toh-nay

Medicines and toiletries

nail varnish
smalto per le unghie
*zmal-toh payr lay **oon**-gyay*

perfume
profumo
*proh-**foo**-moh*

powder
cipria
***chee**-pree-a*

razor blades
lamette
*la-**mayt**-tay*

sanitary towels
assorbenti
*as-sohr-**bayn**-tee*

shampoo
shampo
***sham**-poh*

shaving cream
schiuma da barba
***skyoo**-ma da **bar**-ba*

skin moisturiser
crema idratante
***kray**-ma i-dra-**tan**-tay*

soap
sapone
*sa-**poh**-nay*

suntan oil
olio solare
*o-lyoh soh-**lah**-ray*

talc
borotalco
*boh-roh-**tal**-koh*

tissues
fazzoletti di carta
*fats-soh-**layt**-tee dee **kar**-ta*

toilet water
acqua di Colonia
***ak**-kwa dee koh-**lo**-nya*

toothpaste
dentifricio
*dayn-tee-**free**-choh*

Shopping for clothes

I am just looking, thank you
Sto solo guardando, grazie
*stoh **soh**-loh gwar-**dan**-doh, **gra**-tsyay*

I do not like it
Non mi piace
*nohn mee **pyah**-chay*

I like — this one
Mi piace — questo
*mee **pyah**-chay — **kwe**-stoh*

— that one there
— quello là
*— **kwayl**-loh la*

— the one in the window
— quello in vetrina
*— **kwayl**-loh een vay-**tree**-na*

— this hat
— questo cappello
*— **kwe**-stoh cap-**pel**-loh*

I like it
Mi piace
*mee **pyah**-chay*

187

Shopping for clothes

I will take it
Lo prendo
*loh **prayn**-doh*

I would like this suit
Vorrei questo vestito
*vor-**re**-ee – **kwe**-stoh vay-**stee**-toh*

I would like one — with a zip
Ne vorrei uno — con la cerniera lampo
*nay vor-**re**-ee **oo**-noh — kohn la chayr-**nye**-ra **lam**-poh*

— without a belt
— senza cintura
*— **sen**-tsa cheen-**too**-ra*

I take a larger shoe size
Ho un numero di scarpe più grande
*oh oon **noo**-may-roh dee **skar**-pay pyoo **gran**-day*

I take continental size 40
Ho il 40
*oh eel kwa-**ran**-ta*

Where are the changing (dressing) rooms?
Dove sono i camerini?
***doh**-vay **soh**-noh ee kam-ay-**ree**-nee*

Where can I try it on?
Dove posso provarlo?
***doh**-vay **pos**-soh proh-**vahr**-loh*

Is it too — long?
E' troppo — lungo?
*e **trop**-poh — **loon**-goh*

> **— short?**
> — corto?
> *— **kohr**-toh*

Is there a full length mirror?
C'è uno specchio intero?
*che **oo**-noh **spek**-kyoh een-**tay**-roh*

Is this all you have?
Non avete altro?
*nohn a-**vay**-tay **al**-troh*

It does not fit
Non mi sta
nohn mee sta

It does not suit me
Non mi sta bene
*nohn mee sta **bay**-nay*

May I see it in daylight?
Lo posso vedere alla luce?
*loh **pos**-soh vay-**day**-ray **al**-la **loo**-chay*

What is it made of?
Di cos'è fatto?
*dee ko-**ze fat**-toh*

Clothes and accessories

Will it shrink?
Si restringerà?
see ray-streen-jay-ra

Is it — guaranteed?
  E' — garantita?
  e — ga-ran-tee-ta

  — drip-dry?
  — lava e indossa?
  — lah-va ay een-dos-sa

  — dry-clean only?
  — solo da lavare a secco?
  — soh-loh da lah-vah-ray a sayk-koh

Is it machine washable?
Si può metterlo in lavatrice?
see pwo mayt-tayr-loh een la-va-tree-chay

Clothes and accessories

acrylic
acrilico
a-kree-lee-koh

belt
cintura
cheen-too-ra

blouse
camicia da donna
ka-mee-cha da don-na

bra
reggiseno
rayj-jee-say-noh

Clothes and accessories

bracelet
braccialetto
bra-cha-layt-toh

brooch
spilla
speel-la

button
bottone
boht-toh-nay

cardigan
gilè
jee-le

overcoat
paltò
pal-to

corduroy
velluto a coste
vayl-loo-toh a ko-stay

denim
tela
tay-la

dress
vestito
vay-stee-toh

dungarees
tutina
too-tee-na

earrings
orecchini
oh-rayk-kee-nee

fur
pelliccia
payl-lee-cha

gloves
guanti
gwan-tee

handbag
borsa
bohr-sa

handkerchief
fazzoletto
fats-soh-layt-toh

hat
cappello
kap-pel-loh

jacket
giacchetta
jak-kayt-ta

Clothes and accessories

jeans
jeans
jeens

jersey
maglione
ma-lyoh-nay

lace
merletto
mayr-layt-toh

leather
cuoio
kwo-yoh

linen
lino
lee-noh

necklace
collana
kohl-lah-na

nightdress
camicia da notte
ka-mee-cha da not-tay

nylon
nylon
na-ee-lohn

panties
mutandine
moo-tan-dee-nay

pendant
pendente
payn-den-tay

petticoat
sottoveste
soht-toh-ve-stay

polyester
poliestere
poh-lee-e-stay-ray

poplin
popelin
poh-pay-leen

pullover
pullover
pool-lo-vayr

purse
borsellino
bohr-sel-lee-noh

pyjamas
pigiama
pee-jah-ma

Clothes and accessories

raincoat
impermeabile
*eem-payr-may-**ah**-bee-lay*

rayon
rayon
***ra**-ee-ohn*

ring
anello
*a-**nel**-loh*

sandals
sandali
***san**-da-lee*

scarf
sciarpa
***shar**-pa*

shirt
camicia
*ka-**mee**-cha*

shorts
pantaloncini
*pan-ta-lohn-**chee**-nee*

silk
seta
***say**-ta*

skirt
gonna
***gon**-na*

slip
slip
zleep

socks
calzini
*kal-**tsee**-nee*

stockings
calze da donna
***kal**-tsay da **don**-na*

suede
camoscio
*ka-**mo**-shoh*

suit (men's)
vestito da uomo
*vay-**stee**-toh da **wo**-moh*

suit (women's)
vestito da donna
*vay-**stee**-toh da **don**-na*

sweater
golf
golf

Clothes and accessories

swimming trunks
calzoncini da bagno
kal-tsohn-chee-nee da ba-nyoh

swimsuit
costume da bagno
koh-stoo-may da ba-nyoh

t-shirt
maglietta
ma-lyayt-ta

terylene
terilene
tay-ree-lay-nay

tie
cravatta
kra-vat-ta

tights
collant
kol-lang

towel
asciugamano
a-shoo-ga-mah-noh

trousers
calzoni
kal-tsoh-nee

umbrella
ombrello
ohm-brel-loh

underpants
mutande da uomo
moo-tan-day da wo-moh

velvet
velluto
vayl-loo-toh

vest
canottiera
ka-noht-tye-ra

wallet
portafoglio
pohr-ta-fo-lyoh

watch
orologio
oh-roh-lo-joh

wool
lana
lah-na

zip
cerniera lampo
chayr-nye-ra lam-poh

Photography

I need a film — for this camera
Ho bisogno — di un rollino per questa macchina
                fotografica
*oh bee-**zoh**-nyoh — dee oon rohl-**lee**-noh payr **kwe**-sta*
              ***mak**-kee-na foh-toh-**graf**-fee-ka*

   — for this camcorder
   — di una cassetta per questa videocamera
   *— dee **oo**-na kas-**sayt**-ta payr **kwe**-sta vee-day-oh-**ka**-*
   may-ra

   — for this cine camera
   — di un film per questa macchina da presa
   *— dee oon feelm payr **kwe**-sta **mak**-kee-na da **pray**-za*

   — for this video camera
   — di una cassetta per questa videocamera
   *— dee **oo**-na kas-**sayt**-ta payr **kwe**-sta vee-day-oh-**ka**-*
   may-ra

Can you develop this film, please?
Può sviluppare questo rollino, per favore?
*pwo zveel-loop-**pah**-ray **kwe**-stoh rohl-**lee**-noh, payr*
 *fa-**voh**-ray*

Photography

I would like this photo enlarged
Vorrei un ingrandimento di questa fotografia
vor-re-ee oon een-gran-dee-mayn-toh dee kwe-sta
  foh-toh-gra-fee-a

I would like two prints of this one
Vorrei due copie di questa
vor-re-ee doo-ay co-pyay dee kwe-sta

When will the photos be ready?
Quando saranno pronte le fotografie?
kwan-doh sa-ran-noh prohn-tay lay foh-toh-gra-fee-ay

I want — a black and white film
  Voglio— un rollino bianco e nero
vo-lyoh — oon rohl-lee-noh byan-koh ay nay-roh

  — a colour print film
  — un rollino a colori
  — *oon rohl-lee-noh a koh-loh-ree*

  — a colour slide film
  — un rollino per diapositive a colori
  — *oon rohl-lee-noh payr dee-a-poh-zee-tee-vay a*
    koh-loh-ree

  — batteries for the flash
  — batterie per il flash
  — *bat-tay-ree-ay payr eel flesh*

Camera repairs

There is something wrong with my camera
La mia macchina fotografica ha qualcosa che non va
*la **mee**-a **mak**-kee-na foh-toh-**gra**-fee-ka a kwal-**ko**-za kay
nohn va*

Where can I get my camera repaired?
Dove posso far riparare la mia macchina fotografica?
***doh**-vay **pos**-soh fahr ree-pa-**rah**-ray la **mee**-a **mak**-kee-na
foh-toh-**gra**-fee-ka*

I am having trouble with my camera
Ho dei problemi con la mia macchina fotografica
*oh **day**-ee proh-**ble**-mee kohn la **mee**-a **mak**-kee-na
foh-toh-**gra**-fee-ka*

The film is jammed
Il rollino è bloccato
*eel rohl-**lee**-noh e blohk-**kah**-toh*

Camera parts

accessory
accessori
*a-chays-**soh**-ree*

blue filter
filtro blu
***feel**-troh bloo*

197

Camera parts

camcorder
videocamera
vee-day-oh-ka-may-ra

cartridge
cartuccia
kar-too-cha

cassette
cassetta
kas-sayt-ta

cine camera
macchina da presa
mak-kee-na da pray-za

distance
distanza
dee-stan-tsa

enlargement
ingrandimento
een-gran-dee-mayn-toh

exposure
esposizione
ay-spoh-zee-tsyoh-nay

exposure meter
esposimetro
ay-spoh-zee-may-troh

filter
filtro
feel-troh

flash bulb
lampadina del flash
lam-pa-dee-na dayl flesh

flash cube
cubo del flash
koo-boh dayl flesh

flash
flash
flesh

focal distance
distanza focale
dee-stan-tsa foh-kah-lay

focus
fuoco
fwo-koh

image
immagine
eeem-mah-jee-nay

in focus
a fuoco
a fwo-koh

lens cover
copriobiettivo
*koh-pree-oh-byayt-**tee**-voh*

lens
obiettivo
*oh-byayt-**tee**-voh*

negative
negativa
*nay-ga-**tee**-va*

out of focus
sfuocata
sfwoh-kah-ta

over-exposed
sovraesposta
*soh-vra-ay-**spoh**-stoh*

picture
fotografia
*foh-toh-gra-**fee**-a*

print
stampa
stam-pa

projector
proiettore
*proh-yayt-**toh**-ray*

red filter
filtro rosso
feel-troh rohs-soh

reel
bobina
*boh-**bee**-naa*

shutter
diaframma
*dee-a-**fram**-ma*

slide
diapositiva
*dee-a-poh-zee-**tee**-va*

transparency
trasparenza
*tra-spa-**ren**-tsa*

tripod
cavalletto
*ka-val-**layt**-toh*

under-exposed
sottoesposta
*soht-toh-ay-**spoh**-sta*

viewfinder
mirino
*mee-**ree**-noh*

At the hairdresser's

wide angle lens
grandangolo
*gran-**dan**-goh-loh*

yellow filter
filtro giallo
***feel**-troh **jal**-loh*

At the hairdresser's

I want a haircut
Vorrei tagliarmi i capelli
*vor-**ray**-ee ta-**lyahr**-mee ee ka-**payl**-lee*

Please cut my hair — short
Per favore mi tagli i capelli — corti
*payr fa-**voh**-ray mee **ta**-lyee ee ka-**payl**-lee — **kohr**-tee*

— **in a fringe**
— con la frangia
— *kohn la **fran**-ja*

— **not too short**
— non troppo corti
— *nohn **trop**-poh **kohr**-tee*

— **fairly short**
— abbastanza corti
— *ab-ba-**stan**-tsa **kohr**-tee*

I would like to make an appointment
Vorrei un appuntamento
*vor-**re**-ee oon ap-poon-ta-**mayn**-toh*

At the hairdresser's

I would like — a perm
    Vorrei — a permanente
  vor-re-ee — la payr-ma-nen-tay

        — my hair dyed
        — tingermi i capelli
        — teen-jayr-mee ee ka-payl-lee

        — my hair streaked
        — farmi delle mesh
        — fahr-mee dayl-lay mesh

        — a shampoo and cut
        — shampo e taglio
        — sham-poh ay ta-lyoh

        — a shampoo and set
        — shampo e messa in piega
        — sham-poh ay mays-sa een pye-ga

        — a blow-dry
        — asciugarli con il fon
        — a-shoo-gahr-lee kohn eel fon

        — a trim
        — una spuntatina
        — oo-na spoon-ta-tee-n

Take a little more off the back
Me li sfoltisca ancora un po' di dietro
may lee sfohl-tee-ska an-koh-ra oon po dee dye-troh

Laundry

Not too much off
Non me li sfoltisca troppo
*nohn may lee sfohl-**tee**-ska **trop**-poh*

That is fine, thank you
Questo va bene, grazie
***kwe**-stoh va **bay**-nay, **gra**-tsyay*

I would like — a conditioner
    Vorrei — una lozione ricostituente
  *vor-**re**-ee — **oo**-na loh-**tsyoh**-nay ree-koh-stee-too-**en**-tay*

        — hair spray
        — della lacca
        — ***dayl**-la **lak**-ka*

The dryer is too hot
Il fon è troppo caldo
*eel fon e **trop**-poh **kal**-doh*

The water is too hot
L'acqua è troppo calda
***lak**-kwa e **trop**-poh **kal**-da*

Laundry

Is there a launderette nearby?
C'è una lavanderia automatica qui vicino?
*che **oo**-na la-van-day-**ree**-a oo-toh-**ma**-tee-ka kwee vee-*
  ***chee**-noh*

How does the machine work?
Come funziona la macchina?
koh-may foon-tsyoh-na la mak-kee-na

Can you—clean this skirt?
  Può—lavare questa gonna?
  pwo—la-vah-ray kwe-sta gon-na

  —clean and press these shirts?
  —lavare e stirare queste camicie?
  —la-vah-ray ay stee-rah-ray kwe-stay ka-mee-chay

  —wash these clothes.
  —lavare questi vestiti
  —la-vah-ray kwe-stee vay-stee-tee

How long will it take?
Quanto ci vorrà?
kwan-toh chee vor-ra

Can you do it quickly?
Lo può fare in fretta?
loh pwo fah-ray een frayt-ta

  This stain is — oil
  Questa macchia è — di olio
  kwe-sta mak-kya e — dee **o**-lyoh

    — blood
    — di sangue
    — dee san-gway

> — **coffee**
> — di caffè
> — *dee kaf-fe*

> — **ink**
> — d'inchiostro
> — *deen-kyo-stroh*

When shall I come back?
Quando posso tornare?
***kwan**-doh **pos**-soh tohr-**nah**-ray*

When will my things be ready?
Quando saranno pronte le mie cose?
***kwan**-doh sa-**ran**-noh **prohn**-tay lay **mee**-ay **ko**-zay*

I will come back — later
Ritorno — più tardi
*ree-**tohr**-noh — pyoo **tar**-dee*

> — **in an hour**
> — fra un'ora
> — *fra oo-**noh**-ra*

I have lost my dry cleaning ticket
Ho perso lo scontrino della pulitura a secco
*oh **per**-soh loh skohn-**tree**-noh **dayl**-la poo-lee-**too**-ra a
  sayk-koh*

General repairs

Would you have a look at this please?
Può darci un'occhiata, per piacere?
*pwo **dahr**-chee oo-nohk-**kyah**-ta, payr pya-**chay**-ray*

Can you repair it?
Lo può riparare?
*loh pwo ree-pa-**rah**-ray*

Have you got a spare part for this?
Ha il pezzo di ricambio?
*a eel **pet**-soh dee ree-**kam**-byoh*

This fabric is — delicate
Questo tessuto è — delicato
*kwe-stoh tays-**soo**-toh e — day-lee-**kah**-toh*

— damaged
— rotto
*— **roht**-toh*

— torn
— strappato
*— strap-**pah**-toh*

This is broken
Questo è rotto
*kwe-stoh e **roht**-toh*

General repairs

Here is the guarantee
Ecco la garanzia
ek-koh la ga-ran-tsee-a

Please send it to this address
Per piacere, lo mandi a quest'indirizzo
payr pya-chay-ray, loh man-dee a kwe-steen-dee-reets-soh

Can you give me — some strong glue?
    Mi può dare — della colla forte?
mee pwo dah-ray — dayl-la col-la fohr-tay

— some string?
— dello spago?
— dayl-lo spah-go

— a needle and thread?
— ago e filo?
— ah-go ay fee-loh

I need new heels on these shoes
Ho bisogno di tacchi sulle scarpe
oh bee-zoh-nyoh dee tak-kee sool-lay skar-pay

I need them in a hurry
Ne ho bisogno in fretta
nay oh bee-zoh-nyoh een frayt-ta

At the post office

Central post offices stay open until 8.00pm to sell stamps. Other services usually close at 1.00pm. Smaller post offices close at 1.00pm or 12 noon on Saturday. Stamps can also be bought from tobacconists.

12 stamps please
Dodici francobolli, per piacere
*doh-dee-chee fran-koh-**bohl**-lee, payr pya-**chay**-ray*

I would like some postage stamps
Vorrei dei francobolli
*vor-**ray**-ee **day**-ee fran-koh-**bohl**-lee*

Can I have a telegram form, please?
Mi può dare il modulo per un telegramma, per piacere?
*mee pwo **dah**-ray eel **mo**-doo-loh payr oon tay-lay-**gram**-ma, payr pya-**chay**-ray*

Can I have six stamps for postcards to Britain?
Mi dà i francobolli per sei cartoline per la Gran Bretagna?
*mee da ee fran-koh-**bohl**-lee payr se-ee kar-toh-**lee**-nay payr la gran bray-**ta**-nya*

How much is a letter to Britain?
Quanto costa una lettera per la Gran Bretagna?
*kwan-toh **koh**-sta **oo**-na **let**-tay-ra - payr la gran bray-**ta**-nya*

Using the telephone

I need to send this by courier
Devo mandarlo per corriere
day-voh man-dahr-loh payr cohr-rye-ray

I want to send a telegram
Voglio mandare un telegramma
vo-lyoh man-dah-ray oon tay-lay-gram-ma

I want to send this by registered mail
Voglio fare una raccomandata
vo-lyoh fah-ray oo-na rak-koh-man-dah-ta

I want to send this parcel
Voglio spedire questo pacco
vo-lyoh spay-dee-ray kwe-stoh pak-koh

When will it arrive?
Quando arriverà?
kwan-doh ar-ree-vay-ra

Using the telephone

When there are six digits they are usually expressed in pairs, so the number 205614 would be spoken as 20-56-14. If you find this difficult to follow in Italian, ask for the numbers to be quoted *cifra per cifra* (digit by digit).

Most public phone boxes now take phone cards. For long calls and for international calls you can use a phone box at the local Società Italiana Posta/Telefoni, or SIP, and pay at the desk afterwards.

I would like to make a reversed charge call

Vorrei fare una telefonata a carico del destinatario

*vor-**re**-ee **fah**-ray **oo**-na tay-lay-foh-**nah**-ta a **ka**-ree-koh*
  *dayl day-stee-na-**tah**-ree-oh*

Can you connect me with the international operator?

Mi può passare l'operatore per le chiamate internazionali?

*mee pwo pas-**sah**-ray lo-payr-a-**toh**-ray payr lay*
  *kee-a-**ma**-tay een-tayr-na-tsyoh-**nah**-lee*

Can I dial direct?

Posso chiamare direttamente?

*pos-soh kya-**mah**-ray dee-rayt-ta-**mayn**-tay*

Can I use the telephone, please?

Posso usare il telefono, per piacere?

*pos-soh oo-**zah**-ray eel tay-**le**-foh-noh, payr pya-**chay**-ray*

I must make a phone call to Britain

Devo telefonare in Gran Bretagna

*day-voh tay-lay-foh-**nah**-ray een gran bray-**ta**-nya*

What is the code for the UK?

Qual'è il prefisso per l'Inghilterra?

*kwa-**le** eel pray-**fees**-soh payr leen-gheel-**ter**-ra*

How do I use the telephone?

Come si usa il telefono?

*koh-may see oo-zah eel tay-**le**-foh-noh*

What you may hear

How much is it to phone to London?
Quanto costa telefonare a Londra?
*kwan-toh **koh**-sta tay-lay-foh-**nah**-ray a **lohn**-dra*

Can I use my credit card?
Posso usare la mia carta di credito?
***pos**-soh oo-**zah**-ray la **mee**-a **kar**-ta dee **cray**-dee-toh*

The number I need is…
Il numero di cui ho bisogno è…
*eel **noo**-may-roh dee **koo**-ee oh bee-**zoh**-nyoh e...*

What is the charge?
Quanto costa?
***kwan**-toh **coh**-sta*

I am sorry. We were cut off
Mi dispiace. E' caduta la linea.
*mee dee-**spyah**-chay. e ka-**doo**-ta la **lee**-nay-a*

Please call me back
Per piacere, mi richiami
*payr pya-**chay**-ray, mee ree-**kyah**-mee*

What you may hear

Il numero non è corretto funziona
*eel **noo**-may-roh nohn e kor-**ret**-toh*
The number is out of order

La faccio parlare con il signor Smith
*la **fa**-choh par-**lah**-ray kohn eel **see**-nyohr Smith*
I am putting you through to Mr Smith

La linea è occupata
*la **lee**-nay-a e ohk-koo-**pah**-ta*
The line is engaged (busy)

Non riesco a parlare con questo numero
*non ree-e-skoh a par-**lah**-ray kohn **kwe**-stoh **noo**-may-roh*
I cannot obtain this number

Per favore, continui
*payr fa-**voh**-ray, kohn-**tee**-noo-ee*
Please go ahead

Sto tentando di metterla in contatto
*stoh tayn-**tan**-doh dee **mayt**-tayr-la een kohn-**tat**-toh*
I am trying to connect you

Changing money

Hours vary greatly. Many banks are open 8.30am to 1.20pm and for 45 minutes in the afternoon (usually 3.15pm to 4.00pm). Most are closed at weekends, but some open on Saturday morning where there's a market. Some banks close (or have limited hours) on Monday.

Can I change these traveller's cheques?
Posso cambiare questi traveller's cheques?
***pos**-soh kam-**byah**-ray **kwe**-stee **tra**-vayl-layrs cheks*

Changing money

Can I contact my bank to arrange for a transfer?
Posso contattare la mia banca per farmi fare un bonifico?
*pos-soh kohn-tat-**tah**-ray la **mee**-a **ban**-ka payr **fahr**-mee
fah-ray oon boh-**nee**-fee-koh*

I would like to cash a cheque with my Eurocheque card
Vorrei cambiare un assegno con la mia carta Eurocheque
*vor-**re**-ee kam-**byah**-ray oon as-**say**-nyoh kohn la **mee**-a
kar-ta ay-oo-roh-**shek***

I would like to obtain a cash advance with my credit card
Vorrei incassare dei soldi attraverso la mia carta di credito
*vor-**re**-ee een-kas-**sah**-ray **day**-ee **sol**-dee at-tra-**ver**-soh la
mee-a **kar**-ta dee **kray**-dee-toh*

Can I use traveller's cheques?
Posso usare dei traveller's cheques?
*pos-soh oo-**zah**-ray **day**-ee **tra**-vayl-layrs cheks*

Has my cash arrived?
Sono arrivati i miei soldi?
*soh-noh ar-ree-**vah**-tee ee mee-**e**-ee **sol**-dee*

Here is my passport
Ecco il passaporto
*ek-koh eel pas-sa-**por**-toh*

This is the name and address of my bank
Questo è il nome e l'indirizzo della mia banca
*kwe-stoh e eel **noh**-me ay leen-dee-**reets**-soh dayl-la **mee**-a
ban-ka*

What is the rate for sterling?
A quanto cambiate le sterline?
*a **kwan**-toh kam-**byah**-tay lay stayr-**lee**-nay*

What is the rate of exchange?
Che cambio fate?
*kay **kam**-byoh **fah**-tay*

What is your commission?
Quanto fate pagare di commissione?
***kwan**-toh **fah**-tay pa-**gah**-ray dee kohm-mees-**syoh**-nay*

HEALTH

What's wrong?

I need a doctor
Ho bisogno di un dottore
oh bee-zoh-nyoh dee oon doht-toh-ray

He has been badly injured
E' gravemente ferito
e grah-vay-mayn-tay fay-ree-toh

He is unconscious
E' svenuto
e zvay-noo-toh

He has burnt himself
Si è scottato
see e skoht-tah-toh

He has dislocated his shoulder
Si è slogato una spalla
see e zloh-gah-toh oo-na spal-la

He is hurt
Si è fatto male
see e fat-toh mah-lay

What's wrong?

I am a diabetic
Sono diabetico
soh-noh dee-a-be-tee-koh

I am ill
Sono ammalato
soh-noh am-ma-lah-toh

I am allergic to penicillin
Sono allergico alla penicillina
soh-noh al-ler-jee-koh al-la pay-nee-cheel-lee-na

I am badly sunburnt
Mi sono bruciato al sole
mee soh-noh broo-chah-toh al soh-lay

I am constipated
Sono stitico
soh-noh stee-tee-koh

I am on the pill
Prendo la pillola
prayn-doh la peel-loh-la

I am pregnant
Sono incinta
soh-noh een-cheen-ta

I cannot sleep
Non riesco a dormire
nohn ree-e-skoh a dohr-mee-ray

What's wrong?

I feel dizzy
Mi gira la testa
*mee **jee**-ra la **te**-sta*

I feel faint
Mi sento svenire
*mee **sen**-toh zvay-**nee**-ray*

I feel nauseous
Ho la nausea
*oh la **na**-oo-zay-a*

I fell
Sono caduto
***soh**-noh ka-**doo**-toh*

I have — a headache
　Ho — mal di testa
　*oh — mal dee **te**-sta*

　　— a sore throat
　　— mal di gola
　　— *mal dee **goh**-la*

　　— earache
　　— male a un orecchio
　　— ***mah**-lay a oon oh-**rayk**-kyoh*

　　— cramp
　　— i crampi
　　— *ee **kram**-pee*

I have a pain here
Mi fa male qui
*mee fa **mah**-lay kwee*

I have a rash here
Ho dei brufoli qui
*oh **day**-ee **broo-foh**-lee kwee*

I have been sick
Ho vomitato
*oh voh-mee-**tah**-toh*

I have been stung
Qualcosa mi ha punto
*kwal-**ko**-za mee a **poon**-toh*

I have cut myself
Mi sono tagliato
*mee **soh**-noh ta-**lyah**-toh*

I have diarrhoea
Ho la diarrea
*oh la dee-ar-**ray**-a*

I have hurt —my arm
Mi sono fatto male —al braccio
*mee **soh**-noh **fat**-toh **mah**-lay —al **bra**-choh*

—my leg
—alla gamba
*—**al**-la **gam**-ba*

217

What's wrong?

I have pulled a muscle
Mi sono stirato un muscolo
*mee **soh**-noh stee-**rah**-toh oon **moo**-skoh-loh*

I have sunstroke
Ho preso un colpo di sole
*oh **pray**-zoh oon **kohl**-poh dee **soh**-lay*

I need some antibiotics
Ho bisogno di antibiotici
*oh bee-**zoh**-nyoh dee an-tee-bee-**o**-tee-chee*

I suffer from high blood pressure
Ho la pressione alta
*oh la prays-**syoh**-nay **al**-ta*

I think I have food poisoning
Penso di aver mangiato qualcosa di guasto
***pen**-soh dee a-**vayr** man-**jah**-toh kwal-**co**-za dee **gwa**-stoh*

It is inflamed here
Qui c'è un'infiammazione
*kwee che oon-een-fyam-ma-**tsyoh**-nay*

It is painful — to walk
Mi fa male — quando cammino
*mee fa **mah**-lay — **kwan**-doh kam-**mee**-noh*

— to breathe
— quando respiro
— ***kwan**-doh ray-**spee**-roh*

— **to swallow**
— quando inghiotto
— *kwan-doh een-gyoht-toh*

My arm is broken
Mi sono rotto il braccio
mee soh-noh roht-toh eel bra-choh

My son has cut himself
Mio figlio si è tagliato
mee-oh fee-lyoh see e tal-yah-toh

My son is ill
Mio figlio è ammalato
mee-oh fee-lyoh e amm-ma-lah-toh

My stomach is upset
Mi fa male lo stomaco
mee fa mah-lay loh sto-ma-koh

My tongue is coated
Ho la lingua sporca
oh la leen-gwa spor-ka

She has a temperature
Ha la febbre
a la feb-bray

She has been bitten
E' stata morsa
e stah-ta mor-sa

What's wrong?

She has sprained her ankle
Si è storta una caviglia
*see e **stor**-ta **oo**-na ka-**vee**-lya*

There is a swelling here
C'è un gonfiore qui
*che oon gohn-**fyoh**-ray kwee*

That hurts
Mi fa male
*mee fa **mah**-lay*

Can I see a doctor?
Posso parlare con un dottore?
***pos**-soh par-**lah**-ray kohn oon doht-**toh**-ray*

I am taking these drugs
Prendo queste medicine
***prayn**-doh **kwe**-stay may-dee-**chee**-nay*

Can you give me a prescription for them?
Mi può fare la ricetta?
*mee pwo **fah**-ray la ree-**chet**-ta*

My blood group is . . .
Il mio gruppo sanguigno è . . .
*eel **mee**-oh **groop**-poh san-**gwee**-nyoh e . . .*

I do not know my blood group
Non so quale sia il mio gruppo sanguigno
*nohn soh **kwah**-lay **see**-a eel **mee**-oh **groop**-poh san-**gwee**-nyoh*

Do I have to go into hospital?
Devo andare in ospedale?
day-voh an-*dah*-ray een oh-spay-*dah*-lay

Do I need an operation?
Ho bisogno di un'operazione?
*oh bee-*zoh*-nyoh dee oo-noh-pay-ra-*tsyoh*-nay*

At the hospital

Here is my E111 form
Questo è il mio modulo E111
kwe-stoh e eel *mee*-oh *mo*-doo-loh ay *chen*-toh-*oon*-dee-chee

How do I get reimbursed?
Come faccio a farmi rimborsare?
koh-may *fa*-choh a *fahr*-mee reem-bohr-*sah*-ray

Must I stay in bed?
Devo stare a letto?
day-voh *stah*-ray a *let*-toh

When will I be able to travel?
Quando potrò viaggiare?
kwan-doh poh-*tro* vyaj-*jah*-ray

Will I be able to go out tomorrow?
Posso uscire domani?
pos-soh oo-*shee*-ray doh-*mah*-nee

Parts of the body

ankle
caviglia
*ka-**vee**-lya*

arm
braccio
***bra**-choh*

back
schiena
***skye**-na*

bone
osso
***os**-soh*

breast
seno
***say**-noh*

cheek
guancia
***gwan**-cha*

chest
petto
***pet**-toh*

ear
orecchio
*oh-**rayk**-kyoh*

elbow
gomito
***goh**-mee-toh*

eye
occhio
***ok**-kyoh*

face
faccia
***fa**-cha*

finger
dito
***dee**-toh*

foot
piede
***pye**-day*

hand
mano
***mah**-noh*

Parts of the body

heart
cuore
kwo-ray

kidney
rene
ray-nay

knee
ginocchio
jee-nok-kyoh

leg
gamba
gam-ba

liver
fegato
fay-ga-toh

lungs
polmoni
pohl-moh-nee

mouth
bocca
bohk-ka

muscle
muscolo
moo-skoh-loh

neck
collo
kol-loh

nose
naso
nah-zoh

skin
pelle
pel-lay

stomach
stomaco
sto-ma-koh

throat
gola
goh-la

wrist
polso
pohl-soh

At the dentist's

I have to see the dentist
Devo andare dal dentista
day-voh an-dah-ray dal dayn-tee-sta

I have a toothache
Ho il mal di denti
oh eel mal dee den-tee

I have broken a tooth
Mi si è rotto un dente
mee see e roht-toh oon den-tay

My false teeth are broken
Mi si è rotta la dentiera
mee see e roht-ta la dayn-tye-ra

Can you repair them?
Può ripararla?
pwo ree-pa-rahr-la

My gums are sore
Mi fanno male le gengive
mee fan-noh mah-lay lay jayn-jee-vay

Are you going to fill it?
Lo deve otturare?
loh day-vay oht-too-rah-ray

Please give me an injection
Mi faccia l'iniezione, per favore
mee fa-cha lee-nyay-tsyoh-nay, payr fa-voh-ray

The filling has come out
E' venuta via l'otturazione
e vay-noo-ta vee-a loht-too-ra-tsyoh-nay

This one hurts
Questo mi fa male
kwe-stoh mee fa mah-lay

Will you have to take it out?
Me lo dovrà toglierle?
mee loh doh-vrah to-lyay-ray

FOR YOUR INFORMATION

Numbers

0	zero	*dze-roh*
1	uno	*oo-noh*
2	due	*doo-ay*
3	tre	*tray*
4	quattro	*kwat-troh*
5	cinque	*cheen-kway*
6	sei	*se-ee*
7	sette	*set-tay*
8	otto	*ot-toh*
9	nove	*noh-vay*
10	dieci	*dye-chee*
11	undici	*oon-dee-chee*
12	dodici	*doh-dee-chee*
13	tredici	*tray-dee-chee*
14	quattordici	*kwat-tor-dee-chee*
15	quindici	*kween-dee-chee*
16	sedici	*say-dee-chee*
17	diciassette	*dee-chas-set-tay*
18	diciotto	*dee-chot-toh*
19	diciannove	*dee-chan-no-vay*
20	venti	*vayn-tee*

Numbers

21	ventuno *vayn-**too**-noh*
22	ventidue *vayn-tee-**doo**-ay*
23	ventitre *vayn-tee-**tray***
24	ventiquattro *vayn-tee-**kwat**-troh*
25	venticinque *vayn-tee-**cheen**-kway*
26	ventisei *vayn-tee-**se**-ee*
27	ventisette *vayn-tee-**set**-tay*
28	ventotto *vayn-**tot**-toh*
29	ventinove *vayn-tee-**noh**-vay*
30	trenta ***trayn**-ta*
40	quaranta *kwa-**ran**-ta*
50	cinquanta *cheen-**kwan**-ta*
60	sessanta *says-**san**-ta*
70	settanta *sayt-**tan**-ta*
80	ottanta *oht-**tan**-ta*
90	novanta *noh-**van**-ta*
100	cento ***chen**-toh*
200	duecento *doo-ay-**chen**-toh*
300	trecento *tray-**chen**-toh*
400	quattrocento *kwat-tro-**chen**-toh*
500	cinquecento *cheen-kway-**chen**-toh*
600	seicento *say-ee-**chen**-toh*
700	settecento *sayt-tay-**chen**-toh*
800	ottocento *oht-toh-**chen**-toh*
900	novecento *noh-vay-**chen**-toh*
1000	mille ***meel**-lay*
2000	duemila *doo-ay-**mee**-la*

Ordinals

3000	tremila	*tray-**mee**-la*
4000	quattromila	*kwat-troh-**mee**-la*
1000000	un milione	*oon mee-**lyoh**-nay*

Ordinals

1st	primo	***pree**-moh*
2nd	secondo	*say-**kohn**-doh*
3rd	terzo	***ter**-tsoh*
4th	quarto	***kwar**-toh*
5th	quinto	***kween**-toh*
xth	esimo	***ay**-zee-moh*

Fractions and percentages

10%	dieci per cento	***dye**-chee payr **chen**-toh*
a half	metà	*may-**ta***
a quarter	un quarto	*oon- **kwar**-toh*
a third	un terzo	*oon **ter**-tsoh*
two thirds	due terzi	***doo**-ay **ter**-tsee*

Days

Saturday	sabato	***sa**-ba-to*
Sunday	domenica	*doh-**may**-nee-ka*
Monday	lunedì	*loo-nay-**dee***

Times of the year

Tuesday	martedì *mar-tay-**dee***
Wednesday	mercoledì *mayr-koh-lay-**dee***
Thursday	giovedì *joh-vay-**dee***
Friday	venerdí *vay-nayr-**dee***

Dates

next Tuesday	martedì prossimo *mar-tay-**dee** pros-see-moh*
next week	la settimana prossima *la sayt-tee-**mah**-na pros-see-ma*
last month	il mese scorso *eel **may**-say **skohr**-soh*
last Tuesday	martedì scorso *mar-tay-**dee** **skohr**-soh*
on Friday	venerdì *vay-nayr-**dee***
today	oggi *oj-jee*
tomorrow	domani *doh-**mah**-nee*
yesterday	ieri *ye-ree*

Times of the year

in spring	in primavera *een pree-ma-**ve**-ra*
in summer	in estate *een ay-**stah**-tay*
in autumn	in autunno *een a-oo-**toon**-noh*
in winter	in inverno *een een-**ver**-noh*
in June	in giugno *een **joo**-nyoh*

The seasons

spring	primavera *pree-ma-**ve**-ra*
summer	estate *ay-**stah**-tay*
autumn	autunno *a-oo-**toon**-noh*
winter	inverno *een-**ver**-noh*

Months

January	gennaio *jayn-**na**-ee-oh*
February	febbraio *fayb-**bra**-ee-oh*
March	marzo ***mar**-tsoh*
April	aprile *a-**pree**-lay*
May	maggio ***maj**-joh*
June	giugno ***joo**-nyoh*
July	luglio ***loo**-lyoh*
August	agosto *a-**goh**-stoh*
September	settembre *sayt-**tem**-bray*
October	ottobre *oht-**toh**-bray*
November	novembre *noh-**vem**-bray*
December	dicembre *dee-**chem**-bray*

Public holidays

New Year's Day, January 1
il giorno di capodanno
*eel **johr**-noh dee ca-po-**dan**-noh*

Epiphany, January 6
l'Epifania
*lay-pee-fa-**nee**-a*

Labour Day, May 1
il primo maggio
*eel **pree**-moh **maj**-joh*

Holy Thursday (Maundy Thursday)
Giovedì Santo
*joh-vay-**dee san**-toh*

Good Friday
Venerdì Santo
*vayn-ayr-**dee san**-toh*

Easter Monday
Pasquetta / Lunedì dell'Angelo
*pa-**skwayt**-ta / loo-nay-**dee** dayl-**an**-je-loh*

All Saint's Day, November 1
Ognissanti
*oh-nyees-**san**-tee*

Feast of the Immaculate Conception, December 8
l'Immacolata Concezione
*leem-ma-koh-**lah**-ta kohn-chay-**tsyoh**-nay*

Feast of the Assumption, August 15
Ferragosto
*fayr-ra-**goh**-stoh*

Colours

Christmas Day, December 25
il giorno di Natale
*na-**tah**-lay*

St Stephen's Day, 26 December
Santo Stefano
***san**-toh **stay**-fa-noh*

Colours

beige	**fawn**
beige	marrone chiaro
bej	*mar-**roh**-nay **kyah**-roh*
black	**gold**
nero	giallo oro
***nay**-roh*	***jal**-loh **o**-roh*
blue	**green**
blu	verde
bloo	***vayr**-day*
brown	**grey**
marrone	grigio
*mar-**roh**-nay*	***gree**-joh*
cream	**mauve**
crema	viola
***kray**-ma*	*vee-**o**-la*

orange
arancione
*a-ran-**choh**-nay*

pink
rosa
***ro**-za*

purple
viola
*vee-**o**-la*

red
rosso
***rohs**-soh*

silver
argento
*ar-**jen**-toh*

tan
marrone chiaro
*mar-**roh**-nay **kyah**-roh*

white
bianco
***byan**-koh*

yellow
giallo
***jal**-loh*

Common adjectives

bad
cattivo
*kat-**tee**-voh*

beautiful
bello
***bel**-loh*

big
grande
***gran**-day*

cheap
a buon mercato / economico
*a bwon mayr-**kah**-to /
e-kon-o-ma-**tee**-ko*

cold
freddo
***frayd**-doh*

difficult
difficile
*deef-**fee**-chee-lay*

Common adjectives

easy
facile
fa-chee-lay

long
lungo
loon-goh

expensive
caro
kah-roh

new
nuovo
nwo-voh

fast
veloce
vay-loh-chay

old
vecchio
vek-kyoh

good
buono
bwo-noh

short
breve
bre-vay

high
alto
al-toh

slow
lento
len-toh

hot
caldo
kal-doh

small
piccolo
peek-koh-loh

little
piccolo
peek-koh-loh

ugly
brutto
broot-toh

Signs and notices

acqua potabile
ak-kwa poh-tah-bee-lay
drinking water

affittasi
af-feet-ta-see
to let/for hire

agenzia di viaggi
a-jayn-tsee-a dee vyaj-jee
travel agency

ambulanza
am-boo-lan-tsa
ambulance

aperto
a-per-toh
open

arrivi
ar-ree-vee
arrivals

ascensore
a-shayn-soh-ray
lift/elevator

attenti al cane
at-ten-tee al kah-nay
beware of the dog

attenzione
at-tayn-tsyoh-nay
caution

bagaglio
ba-ga-lyoh
baggage

banca
ban-ka
bank

benvenuto
bayn-vay-noo-toh
welcome

caldo
kal-doh
hot

cassa
kas-sa
cash desk

Signs and notices

chiuso
kyoo-zoh
closed

dogana
doh-ga-na
Customs

emergenza
ay-mayr-jen-tsa
emegency

entrata
ayn-trah-ta
entrance

esaurito
ay-za-oo-ree-toh
sold out

freddo
frayd-doh
cold

immondizia
eem-mohn-dee-tsee-a
litter

in vendita
een vayn-dee-ta
for sale

informazioni
een-fohr-ma-tsyoh-nee
information

ingresso libero
een-gres-soh lee-bay-roh
no admission charge

libero
lee-bay-roh
vacant

liquidazione
lee-kwee-da-tsyoh-nay
sale

lista dei prezzi
lee-sta day-ee pret-tsee
price list

non toccare
nohn tohk-kah-ray
do not touch

occupato
ohk-koo-pah-toh
occupied

offerta speciale
ohf-fer-ta spay-chah-lay
special offer

orario
*oh-**rah**-ree-oh*
timetable

ospedale
*oh-spay-**dah**-lay*
hospital

partenze
*par-**ten**-tsay*
departure

pericolo
*pay-**ree**-koh-loh*
danger

polizia
*poh-lee-**tsee**-a*
police

pomeriggio chiuso
*poh-may-**reej**-joh **kyoo**-zoh*
closed in the afternoon

pompieri
*pohm-**pye**-ree*
fire brigade

prenotato
*pray-noh-**ta**-toh*
reserved

scuola
skwo-la
school

signore
*see-**nyoh**-ray*
ladies

signori
*see-**nyoh**-ree*
gentlemen

souvenir
*soov-**neer***
souvenirs

spingere
***speen**-jay-ray*
push

suonare
*swoh-**nah**-ray*
ring

telefono
*tay-**le**-foh-noh*
telephone

tirare
*tee-**rah**-ray*
pull

237

Signs and notices

uscita d'emergenza
oo-shee-ta day-mayr-jen-tsa
emergency exit

uscita
oo-shee-ta
exit

veleno
vay-lay-noh
poison

vietato entrare
vyay-tah-toh
ayn-trah-ray
no trespassing

vietato fotografare
vyay-tah-toh foh-toh-gra-
fah-ray
no photographs

vietato fumare
vyay-tah-toh foo-mah-ray
no smoking

vietato sporgersi
vyay-tah-toh spor-jayr-see
do not lean out

pericolo d'incendio
pay-ree-koh-loh deen-chen-
dyoh
danger of fire

pericolo di morte
pay-ree-koh-loh dee mor-tay
danger of death

riservato a . . .
ree-zayr-va-to a . . .
allowed only for . . .

allarme antincendio
al-lahr-may an-teen-chen-
dyoh
fire alarm

per favore suonare
payr fa-voh-ray swoh-nah-ray
please ring

entrare senza bussare
ayn-trah-ray sen-tsa boos-
sah-ray
enter without knocking

svendita per fine
zvayn-dee-ta payr fee-nay ay-
sayr-chee-tsyoh
closing down sale

ufficio oggetti smarriti
*oof-**fee**-choh oj-**jet**-tee zmar-**ree**-tee*
lost property office

è proibito calpestare l'erba
*e proh-ee-**bee**-toh kal-pay-**stah**-ray **ler**-ba*
keep off the grass

solo per uso esterno
*soh-loh payr **oo**-zoh ay-**ster**-noh*
for external use only

è proibito parlare al conducente mentre il bus è in movimento
*e proh-ee-**bee**-toh par-**lah**-ray al kohn-doo-**chen**-tay **mayn**-tray eel boos e een moh-vee-**mayn**-toh*
It is forbidden to speak to the driver while the bus is moving

riservato al personale
*ree-zayr-**vah**-toh al payr-soh-**nah**-lay*
staff only

In an Emergency

Dial 113 for the *polizia*, *pompieri* or *ambulanza*.

There are several categories of police and their roles sometimes overlap. The *carabinieri* are military police concerned with public order. They are the highest grade of police and are always armed. The *polizia* have several sections – if someone is hurt in a road accident you should inform the *polizia stradale* (113). The *vigili urbani* ('town watch') see that bye-laws and civic rules are adhered to.

Call an ambulance
Chiamate un'ambulanza
*kya-**mah**-tay oo-nam-boo-**lan**-tsa*

Call the fire brigade
Chiamate i pompieri
*kya-**mah**-tay ee pohm-**pye**-ree*

Call the police
Chiami la polizia
***kyah**-mee la poh-lee-**tsee**-a*

There is a fire
C'è un incendio
*che oon een-**chen**-dyoh*

Get a doctor
Chiami un dottore
***kyah**-mee oon doht-**toh**-ray*

Where is — the British consulate?
Dov'è — il consolato inglese?
*doh-**ve** — eel kohn-soh-**la**-toh een-**glay**-zay*

— the police station?
— la centrale di polizia?
*— la chayn-**trah**-lay dee poh-leet-**see**-a*